D0430980

Daniel
GOD'S PATTERN FOR THE FUTURE

BIBLE STUDY GUIDE

From the Bible-teaching ministry of

Charles R. Swindoll

INSIGHT FOR LIVING

These studies are based on the outlines of sermons delivered by Charles R. Swindoll. Chuck is a graduate of Dallas Theological Seminary and has served in pastorates for over twenty-two years, including churches in Texas, New England, and California. Since 1971 he has served as senior pastor of the First Evangelical Free Church of Fullerton, California. Chuck's radio program, "Insight for Living," began in 1979. In addition to his church and radio ministries, Chuck has authored twenty books and numerous booklets on a variety of subjects.

Chuck's outlines are expanded from the sermon transcripts and edited by Bill Watkins, a graduate of California State University at Fresno and Dallas Theological Seminary, with the assistance of Bill Butterworth, a graduate of Florida Bible College, Dallas Theological Seminary, and Florida Atlantic University. Bill Watkins is presently the director of educational resources, and Bill Butterworth is currently the director of counseling ministries at Insight for Living.

Creative Director:	Cynthia Swindoll
Editor:	Bill Watkins
Associate Editor:	Bill Butterworth
Copy Supervisor:	Wendy Jones
Editorial Assistants:	Glenda Gardner, Jane Gillis, and Julie Martin
Director, Communications Division:	Carla Beck
Project Supervisor:	Alene Cooper
Art Director:	Ed Kesterson
Production Artist:	Becky Englund
Typographers:	Bob Haskins and Debbie Krumland
Calligrapher:	Richard Stumpf
Cover:	Painting by Briton Riviere, *Daniel's Answer to the King*
Production Supervisor:	Deedee Snyder
Printer:	R. R. Donnelley & Sons Co.

An album that contains eighteen messages on nine cassettes and corresponds to this study guide may be purchased through Insight for Living, Post Office Box 4444, Fullerton, California 92634. For ordering information and a current catalog, please write our offices or call (714) 870-9161.

Canadian residents may obtain a catalog and ordering information through Insight for Living Ministries, Post Office Box 2510, Vancouver, British Columbia, Canada V6B 3W7, (604) 272-5811. Overseas residents should direct their correspondence to our Fullerton office.

If you wish to order by Visa or MasterCard, you are welcome to use our toll-free number, (800) 772-8888, Monday through Friday between the hours of 8:30 A.M. and 4:00 P.M., Pacific Time. This number may be used anywhere in the continental United States excluding Alaska, California, and Hawaii. Orders from those areas can be made by calling our general office number, (714) 870-9161.

Unless otherwise identified, all Scripture references are from the New American Standard Bible, © The Lockman Foundation 1960, 1962, 1963, 1968, 1971, 1972, 1973, 1975, 1977. Used by permission.

© 1976, 1980, 1986 by Charles R. Swindoll. All rights reserved. Printed in the United States of America. No portion of this publication may be reproduced in any form, except for brief quotations in reviews, without prior written permission of the publisher, Insight for Living, Post Office Box 4444, Fullerton, California 92634.

ISBN 0-8499-8219-7

Table of Contents

Daniel
God's Pattern for the Future

*Daniel, the prophet, could be called a man for all seasons.
He "stood in the gap" through one pagan ruler after another,
never once compromising his convictions. As one in great
authority, Daniel certainly had opportunities to fudge
morally, spiritually, and ethically . . . but that peerless
model of integrity never did.*

*These studies, however, are about more than the man
himself. They also deal with some of the most colorful and
significant prophetic themes found in Scripture. What the
book of Revelation is to the New Testament, Daniel is to
the Old. With sweeping, broad brush strokes of his pen,
Daniel covers the major areas of prophecy.*

*As you read each lesson in this study guide, with your Bible
open to this great book, may God stimulate and strengthen
you. My hope is that you will do more than just learn about
a few interesting events regarding the future, important
though they may be . . . but that Daniel's example of
integrity will mark your life in a permanent manner.*

Chuck Swindoll

Putting Truth into Action

Knowledge apart from application falls short of God's desire for His children. Knowledge must result in change and growth. Consequently, we have constructed this Bible study guide with these purposes in mind: (1) to stimulate discovery, (2) to increase understanding, and (3) to encourage application.

At the end of each lesson is a section called 🖼️ *Living Insights. There you'll be given assistance in further Bible study, thoughtful interaction, and personal appropriation. This is the place where the lesson is fitted with shoe leather for your walk through the varied experiences of life.*

In wrapping up some lessons, you'll find a unit called 🖼️ *Digging Deeper. It will provide you with essential information and list helpful resource materials so that you can probe further into some of the issues raised in those studies.*

It's our hope that you'll discover numerous ways to use this tool. Some useful avenues we would suggest are personal meditation, joint discovery, and discussion with your spouse, family, work associates, friends, or neighbors. The study guide is also practical for church classes and, of course, as a study aid for the "Insight for Living" radio broadcast. The individual studies can usually be completed in thirty minutes. However, some are more open-ended and could be expanded for greater depth. Their use is flexible!

In order to derive the greatest benefit from this process, we suggest that you record your responses to the lessons in a notebook where writing space is plentiful. In view of the kinds of questions asked, your notebook may become a journal filled with your many discoveries and commitments. We anticipate that you will find yourself returning to it periodically for review and encouragement.

Bill Watkins
Editor

Bill Butterworth
Associate Editor

Daniel

GOD'S PATTERN FOR THE FUTURE

Prophecy in Panorama
Selected Scripture

Our modern world suffers from a population explosion, civil and international upheaval, nation-sweeping famines, devastating earthquakes, and deceitful cults. In such a setting, Christ's prophetic words ring with relevance:

> "Many will come in My name, saying, 'I am the Christ,' and will mislead many. And you will be hearing of wars and rumors of wars; see that you are not frightened, for those things must take place, but that is not yet the end. For nation will rise against nation, and kingdom against kingdom, and in various places there will be famines and earthquakes. But all these things are merely the beginning of birth pangs." (Matt. 24:5–8)

We are definitely in the "last days" (2 Tim. 3:1, 2 Pet. 3:3). The Lord is bringing to a close another stage of His redemptive plan in history. And He has not left us in the dark concerning His present and future strategy; He has revealed His plan throughout Scripture. Among the Bible's books of prophecy, Daniel is one of the most prominent. Let's take a close look at this Old Testament document and carefully consider its relevance to our lives. We will begin by gaining a panoramic view of God's prophesied program in human history.

I. Some Introductory Matters

Scanning the contemporary scene, we can make at least two observations with regard to prophecy. First, *there is a great hunger for prophetic information.* Newsstands and bookstores are filled with material that contains predictions about the future. Musicals and movies frequently present scenarios of what tomorrow may hold. Even the rise in the number of fortune-tellers and spiritual mediums indicates that people are extremely anxious to get a glimpse into the future. Second, *there is a great imbalance among many students of prophecy.* These individuals tend to carry the study of the subject to extremes and, in the process, frequently arrive at unsound conclusions. For example, some have set dates concerning such

1

events as the Rapture and the Second Advent. But Jesus said that only the Heavenly Father knows when certain end-time happenings will occur (Matt. 24:36). In fact, Jesus told His disciples that it was not for them " 'to know times or epochs which the Father has fixed by His own authority' " (Acts 1:7). The same is true for us. We need to strive for balance and humility in our study of biblical prophecy. Along with these observations, there is one more item that we should note: *There are two great books of prophecy in Scripture—Daniel and Revelation.* The prophecy in the Book of Daniel focuses primarily on the Gentiles, whereas the nation of Israel is the central subject of the prophecy in Revelation.

II. God's Overall Scheme

We will gain a better understanding of the prophesied program revealed in Daniel by surveying God's overall plan in history. The chart found at the end of this lesson illustrates much of what is explained in the points that follow. Even though we will not cover all the major stages of God's dealings with man, we will see some that are especially important to our study of Daniel.

A. The Law. Some time after their creation, the first human couple violated God's command and brought death to the human race (Gen. 3, Rom. 5:12). Even before the Lord created anything, He knew that man would abuse his freedom of choice. He also knew what steps He would take to provide for man's deliverance from the penalty of sin. One of the earliest stages in this redemptive plan was the revelation of the Law through the prophet Moses (Exod. 19–31). Although the Law was not given as a means of salvation, it did expose man's sinfulness and his need to be saved by grace through faith in the Savior (Rom. 3:19–20, Gal. 3:19–24). The Law also provided a standard by which the nation of Israel could regulate its religious and social behavior. Unfortunately, the Israelites did not faithfully obey the Mosaic Law. Consequently, their nation suffered religious and political turmoil that led to its division into two kingdoms—Israel and Judah—in 931 B.C. Both of these nations were eventually defeated by foreign armies—Israel was conquered by Assyria around 722 B.C., and Judah was defeated by Babylon about 586 B.C. The Hebrew prophet Daniel lived between 605 and 530 B.C. He wrote the book that bears his name after the defeat of Judah and while he and his fellow countrymen were exiled in Babylonia. However, God, in His grace, did not allow the Israelites to remain in bondage. After they had spent seventy years in exile, the Lord provided a way for the Hebrews to return to their native land and begin rebuilding Jerusalem (see the

Books of Ezra and Nehemiah).[1] Soon after this deliverance, the Israelites again rebelled against God and, as a result, received no more prophetic revelation for four hundred years. This period of divine silence is known as the intertestamental period.[2] It came to an end with the birth announcements of John the Baptist and Jesus Christ (Luke 1). These individuals lived, ministered, and died under the Mosaic Law. Christ's resurrection from the grave, however, signaled that a new stage in God's plan was about to begin.

B. The Church. None of the Old Testament saints foresaw the Church Age. It was hidden from them by God and revealed by Him primarily through the Apostle Paul (Eph. 3:2–11). The beginning of the Church Age is recorded in Acts 2, where we read that on the day of Pentecost following Christ's ascension into heaven the apostles were filled with the Holy Spirit and enabled to speak in tongues. From this point on, the apostles understood that God was performing a new work among the Jews. But it was some time later when they realized that the Lord was including non-Jews—the Gentiles—in the Church as well (Acts 10:1–11:18). During this stage in God's prophesied program, there is no distinction between Jew and Gentile. Everyone who accepts Jesus Christ as Savior by faith becomes an equal member of God's everlasting family and thereby an heir of His promises—even of those made to Israel (Gal. 3:28–29, Eph. 3:6). Furthermore, we can discern from Scripture that the age of the Church will end when the Rapture occurs. God has not revealed the date of this event. However, Christ has promised that His Church will never be overpowered and defeated (Matt. 16:18).

1. More information on Israel's history can be found in these sources: F. F. Bruce, *Israel and the Nations* (London: Paternoster Press, 1963); Leon Wood, *A Survey of Israel's History* (Grand Rapids, Mich.: Zondervan Publishing House, 1970); John H. Walton, *Chronological and Background Charts of the Old Testament,* foreword by Merrill C. Tenney (Grand Rapids, Mich.: Academie Books, Zondervan Publishing House, 1978); and Edwin R. Thiele, *The Mysterious Numbers of the Hebrew Kings,* rev. ed. (Grand Rapids, Mich.: Zondervan Publishing House, 1983). An insightful account of contemporary events surrounding Israel is provided by former President Jimmy Carter in his book *The Blood of Abraham* (Boston: Houghton Mifflin Co., 1985).

2. The intertestamental period provides a rich area of study for students of the Bible. If you would like to learn more about this period, we recommend that you consult these sources: Roy A. Stewart and Robert J. Wyatt, "Intertestamental Period," in *The International Standard Bible Encyclopedia,* 4 vols., rev. ed. (Grand Rapids, Mich.: William B. Eerdmans Publishing Co., 1979, 1982, 1986), vol. 2, pp. 874–78; F. F. Bruce, *New Testament History* (Garden City, N.Y.: Anchor Books, 1972); Harold W. Hoehner, *Herod Antipas* (Grand Rapids, Mich.: Zondervan Publishing House, 1972); and W. G. Hardy, *The Greek and Roman World,* rev. ed. (Cambridge, Mass.: Schenkman Publishing Co., 1970).

C. The Rapture. At some unspecified time in the future,

> The Lord Himself will descend from heaven with a shout, with the voice of the archangel, and with the trumpet of God; and the dead in Christ shall rise first. Then we [Christians] who are alive and remain shall be caught up together with them in the clouds to meet the Lord in the air, and thus we shall always be with the Lord. (1 Thess. 4:16–17)

In other words, all those who place their trust in Christ as Savior from the day of Pentecost (Acts 2) to the moment just before the Rapture will join Christ in the air. First Corinthians 15 tells us that "in the twinkling of an eye" all the participants in the Rapture will receive imperishable, immortal bodies (vv. 50–53). Of course, one consequence of this event is that only non-Christians will be left on earth. This will mark the beginning of another stage in God's prophesied program.[3]

D. The Great Tribulation. The most terrifying and destructive period of sin and judgment recorded in Scripture is the Tribulation. During this seven-year span, the dominant personality and major political figure will be a man the Bible refers to as "the beast" (Rev. 13:1–8). His right-hand man will be a false prophet, whom Scripture also calls a beast (vv. 11–17). Both of these individuals will utilize deception and satanic power in an attempt to control the world politically, economically, and religiously. Those who exercise their faith in Christ during this period will be mercilessly persecuted. Many will even be killed as a result of their Christian convictions. But the Lord will not allow this evil to persist. During the Tribulation period, God will unleash His anger in a series of devastating judgments that will culminate in the Battle of Armageddon (Rev. 6–18).

E. The Second Advent. The return of Christ will occur when the armies of the world are assembled for battle at the plain of Armageddon. The Bible says that Jesus Christ will descend from heaven "clothed with a robe dipped in blood" and riding on a "white horse" (19:13, 11). Accompanying Him will be all the Christians who were raptured before the Tribulation began (v. 14; cf. vv. 1–10). He will seize the beast and the false prophet and throw them "alive into the lake of fire which burns with brimstone" (v. 20). Then Christ will kill all those who sided with the beast during the Tribulation period, and He will bind Satan for a thousand years (vv. 19, 21; 20:1–3).

---

3. The Rapture and its relationship to the Tribulation are discussed in the study guide *Contagious Christianity: A Study of First Thessalonians,* edited by Bill Watkins, from the Bible-teaching ministry of Charles R. Swindoll (Fullerton, Calif.: Insight for Living, 1985), pp. 44–56.

F. The Millennial Kingdom. Following the Battle of Armageddon, Christ will initiate a thousand-year reign of righteousness on earth. Only believers will enter this perfect environment, but not all of the children born during this time will trust in Christ. In fact, when Satan is freed toward the end of Jesus' millennial rule, he will deceive those who have not placed their faith in Christ and "gather them together for the war" against "the saints and the beloved city [i.e., Jerusalem]" (20:7–9a). But the Lord will destroy these unbelievers, and He will cast Satan "into the lake of fire and brimstone, where the beast and the false prophet are also; and they will be tormented day and night forever and ever" (vv. 9b–10). Then God will resurrect all of the unsaved, judge them "according to their deeds," and throw them "into the lake of fire" (vv. 11–15).

G. The New Creation. With evil finally defeated, God will destroy the old heaven and earth and re-create "new heavens and a new earth, in which righteousness [will dwell]" (2 Pet. 3:13; cf. vv. 10–12, Rev. 21:1). In this new world, the Lord " 'shall wipe away every tear from [His people's] eyes; and there shall no longer be any death; there shall no longer be any mourning, or crying, or pain' " (Rev. 21:4). Christ will rule in an environment completely free from evil and its effects. And all those who trusted in Him for their salvation will live forever in bliss.

III. Daniel's Specific Scope

We will discover in our study that the author of the Book of Daniel was unaware of God's full prophetic plan. As far as we know, the prophet Daniel only had knowledge of five key prophetic events: (1) the rise of Gentile supremacy, (2) the rebuilding of Jerusalem, (3) the coming and death of the Messiah, (4) the Great Tribulation, and (5) the Millennial Kingdom. Of course, the first three events have already occurred in history; however, the last two are yet to come. There are a couple more observations we need to make about Daniel's understanding. First, his major focus is the Gentiles. And second, the major sources of his message are dreams and visions.

IV. Our Basic Response

If you are not a Christian, please pay heed to what the Book of Daniel has to say. Its message is as relevant to you as it is to anyone else. If you are a believer, find comfort in the prophecies of this book. They make it clear that no matter how bleak the circumstances appear to be, the Lord is in control, and He will carry out His good purpose in His perfect time.

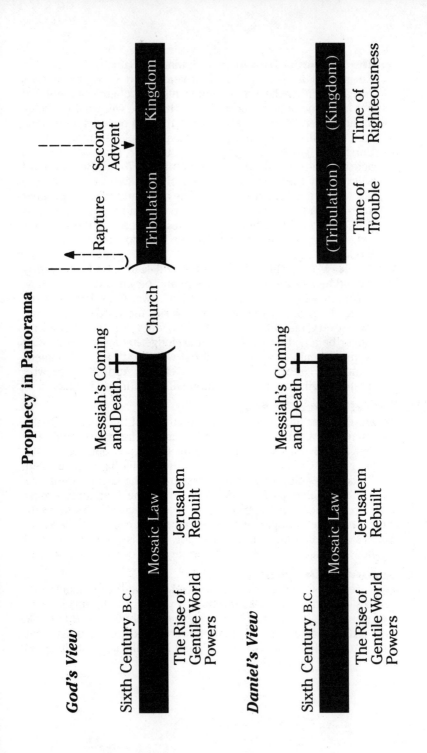

Prophecy in Panorama

God's View

Sixth Century B.C.

The Rise of Gentile World Powers

Mosaic Law

Jerusalem Rebuilt

Messiah's Coming and Death

Church

Rapture

Tribulation

Second Advent

Kingdom

Daniel's View

Sixth Century B.C.

The Rise of Gentile World Powers

Mosaic Law

Jerusalem Rebuilt

Messiah's Coming and Death

(Tribulation)

(Kingdom)

Time of Trouble

Time of Righteousness

6

⚙️ *Living Insights*

There's something very helpful about getting an *overview*. It offers a panoramic perspective of where we were, where we are, and where we are going. Let's use this exercise to get better acquainted with God's overall scheme.

● Copy the following charts into your notebook. Using the Scriptures listed, write down some observations about the Law, the Church, and the Rapture. We will look at three other major periods of God's program for mankind in the next Living Insights.

The Law	
References	Observations
Exodus 19–23	
Exodus 25–31	

The Church	
References	Observations
Matthew 16:18	
Acts 2	
1 Corinthians 12:12–13	
Ephesians 1–3	

The Rapture	
References	Observations
John 14:1–3	
1 Corinthians 15:50–58	
1 Thessalonians 4:13–18	
Revelation 3:10	

Continued on next page

🐎 *Living Insights*

In our first study, we overviewed several key stages of God's plan in human history. For example, we recalled the origin and end of the period of Law, reviewed crucial aspects of the present Church Age, and looked forward to the Rapture. Let's go back to the future part of God's program and zero in on three major events.

● After copying these charts, look up the Scriptures listed in each section. As you read these passages, write down pertinent details referring to the Tribulation, the Second Advent of Christ, and the Millennial Kingdom. This exercise will deepen your understanding of God's plan for the future.

The Tribulation	
References	Observations
Daniel 7, 9:26–27, 11 Matthew 24:15–28 Revelation 6–18	

The Second Advent	
References	Observations
Matthew 24:29–31 Revelation 19:11–21	

The Millennial Kingdom	
References	Observations
Isaiah 11, 60–66 Daniel 12 Revelation 20	

🗹 *Digging Deeper*

The interpretation of biblical prophecy given in this lesson is a *premillennial* one. That is, we believe that the promises God made to Israel will be completely fulfilled in an earthly one-thousand-year reign of Christ that will begin after Jesus returns in power and judgment. However, not all Christians accept this understanding of the scriptural record. Some maintain that "the kingdom of God is now being extended in the world through the preaching of the gospel and the saving work of the Holy Spirit in the hearts of individuals, that the world eventually is to be Christianized and that the return of Christ is to occur at the close of a long period of righteousness and peace commonly called the millennium."[4] This view is called *postmillennialism*. Still others think that we are in the "millennium" now. They do not believe that this period is literally one thousand years in length or that it involves an actual earthly reign of Christ. Rather, they contend that we are presently reaping the benefits associated with the Millennium and that we will continue to do so progressively until Christ returns. At that time He will resurrect believers, transforming them to immortal life, and resurrect and judge unbelievers, sentencing them to everlasting corruption. This position is known as *amillennialism*. If you would like to probe further into the arguments for and against each of these interpretations, we suggest that you refer to the materials which follow.

● **Sources on the Interpretation of the Millennium**

Adams, Jay Edward. *I Tell You the Mystery*. Lookout Mountain, Tenn.: Prospective Press, 1966. Amillennial.

Allis, Oswald T. *Prophecy and the Church*. Reprint. Grand Rapids, Mich.: Baker Book House, 1977. Amillennial.

Boettner, Loraine. *The Millennium*. Philadelphia: Presbyterian and Reformed Publishing Co., 1957. Postmillennial.

Campbell, Roderick. *Israel and the New Covenant*. Reprint. Philadelphia: Presbyterian and Reformed Publishing Co., 1982. Postmillennial.

Clouse, Robert G., ed. *The Meaning of the Millennium: Four Views*. Downers Grove, Ill.: InterVarsity Press, 1977. This book contains essays by, and interactions between, four Christian scholars on historic premillennialism, dispensational premillennialism, postmillennialism, and amillennialism.

Cox, William E. *Amillennialism Today*. Philadelphia: Presbyterian and Reformed Publishing Co., 1972. Amillennial.

Feinberg, Charles L. *Millennialism: The Two Major Views*. Reprint. Chicago: Moody Press, 1980. Premillennial.

Kik, J. Marcellus. *An Eschatology of Victory*. Nutley, N. J.: Presbyterian and Reformed Publishing Co., 1974. Postmillennial.

Ladd, George E. *The Last Things*. Grand Rapids, Mich.: William B. Eerdmans Publishing Co., 1978. Premillennial.

---

4. Anthony A. Hoekema, "Amillennialism," in *The Meaning of the Millennium: Four Views*, edited by Robert G. Clouse (Downers Grove, Ill.: InterVarsity Press, 1977), p. 117.

McClain, Alva J. *The Greatness of the Kingdom.* Grand Rapids, Mich.: Zondervan Publishing House, 1959. Premillennial.

Ridderbos, Herman Nicholas. *The Coming of the Kingdom.* Philadelphia: Presbyterian and Reformed Publishing Co., 1962. Amillennial.

Shedd, William G. T. *Dogmatic Theology.* 4 vols. Reprint. Minneapolis: Klock and Klock Christian Publishers, 1979. Vol. 2A. Postmillennial.

Walvoord, John F. *The Millennial Kingdom.* Grand Rapids, Mich.: Zondervan Publishing House, 1959. Premillennial.

How to Pass a Test without Cheating
Daniel 1

Throughout history, foreign armies have invaded nations, taking people captive and transporting them to unfamiliar territory. Tragically, this action usually separates family members from one another—sometimes for a lifetime. As far as we know, Daniel was taken from his family by a Babylonian military leader who besieged Jerusalem in the seventh century B.C. As a young boy, Daniel was uprooted from his native land of Judah and planted in the wicked soil of Babylon. Many of his experiences in this foreign land are recorded in the Bible book that bears his name. As we study its pages, we will learn a great deal about God and how we should respond to Him, to His strategy in human history, and to those with whom we come in contact. Let's open our hearts to the timeless message of this ancient book.

I. The Historical Setting

Daniel 1:1–2 tells us, "In the third year of the reign of Jehoiakim king of Judah, Nebuchadnezzar king of Babylon came to Jerusalem and besieged it. And the Lord gave Jehoiakim king of Judah into his hand, along with some of the vessels of the house of God; and he brought them to the land of Shinar, to the house of his god, and he brought the vessels into the treasury of his god." These events occurred in early 605 B.C., soon after the Battle of Carchemish that was fought between the Euphrates and Orontes rivers. Nebuchadnezzar almost annihilated the Egyptian army during this conflict, signaling the rise of Babylonia as the new world power. As a result of this victory, the land to the south of Babylonia, namely, "all Syria and Palestine to the border of Egypt, now lay exposed to the new conqueror. All he had to do was assert control, which he began doing immediately, moving as far south as Jerusalem, where he forced the submission of Jehoiakim and other kings of the area."[1] But, as Old Testament scholar Leon Wood points out, Nebuchadnezzar was not content with having the leading cities of these lands under his control. He also desired "the procurement of able young men, whom he might relocate in Babylon as prospective government personnel. It is likely that each city was forced to give him their finest. Among those from Jerusalem were Daniel and his three friends, Hananiah, Mishael, and Azariah."[2] We know from extrabiblical historical records that Nebuchadnezzar's wartime activities were cut short when he received the news that his ailing

1. Leon Wood, *A Survey of Israel's History* (Grand Rapids, Mich.: Zondervan Publishing House, 1970), p. 373.

2. Wood, *Survey of Israel's History,* p. 373.

father, Nabopolassar, had died. Consequently, in August of 605 B.C., Nebuchadnezzar returned to Babylon in order to be crowned Nebuchadnezzar II, king of Babylonia, bringing with him captives and material goods.[3] Historian and archaeologist Howard F. Vos describes the magnificence of this city in these words:

> Adjacent to Nebuchadnezzar's main palace and just to the east of it was the great Ishtar gate, through which passed Procession Street, the main street of the city. In honor of [the god] Marduk, this roadway was paved with imported limestone and sometimes reached a width of sixty-five feet. It was bordered with sidewalks of red breccia. Walls on either side of the road were faced with blue enameled brick and decorated with life-size yellow and white lions and dragons. The city's major structures opened on this roadway. The Ishtar gate was a double gate flanked with towers of blue enameled brick decorated with alternating rows of yellow and white bulls and dragons. Nebuchadnezzar's palace was a huge complex of buildings protected by a double wall. Rooms of the palace surrounded five courtyards. The white plastered throne room (56 by 170 feet) had a great central entrance flanked by smaller side doors.
>
> The city itself, roughly rectangular, sat astride the Euphrates. The wall, 11 miles long and 85 feet thick, was protected by a moat filled with water from the Euphrates. Actually the wall was double; the outer wall was 25 feet thick and the inner one 23 feet thick with an intervening space filled with rubble. Watchtowers stood 65 feet apart on the walls. There were eight or nine gates in the wall, with the Ishtar gate entering from the north. As mentioned, the palace of Nebuchadnezzar, the ziggurat, and the great temple of Marduk all opened off Procession Street. Altogether there were forty-three temples in the city of Nebuchadnezzar's day.... The population of greater Babylon in the sixth century B.C. has been estimated at about a half million.[4]

A visual layout of Babylon and several of its major sights is provided on the facing page.

---

3. Wood, *Survey of Israel's History,* p. 373.

4. Howard F. Vos, *Archaeology in Bible Lands* (Chicago: Moody Press, 1977), p. 115. More information on Babylon can be found in Alan Millard's book *Treasures from Bible Times* (Belleville, Mich.: Lion Publishing Corp., 1985), pp. 134–40, and in the article by Donald J. Wiseman titled "Babylon," in *The International Standard Bible Encyclopedia,* 4 vols., rev. ed. (Grand Rapids, Mich.: William B. Eerdmans Publishing Co., 1979, 1982, 1986), vol. 1, pp. 384–91.

The Great Babylon—Capital of Babylonia

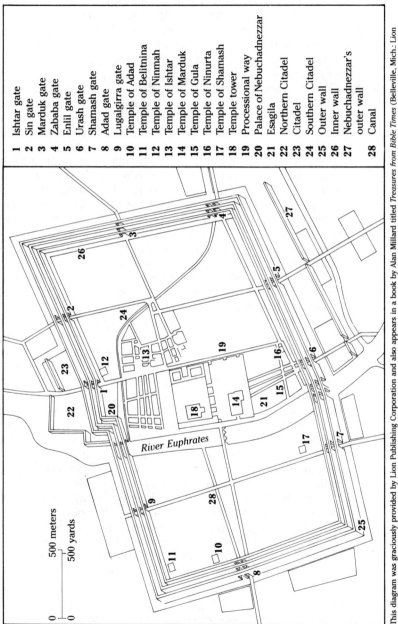

1 Ishtar gate
2 Sin gate
3 Marduk gate
4 Zababa gate
5 Enlil gate
6 Urash gate
7 Shamash gate
8 Adad gate
9 Lugalgirra gate
10 Temple of Adad
11 Temple of Belitnina
12 Temple of Ninmah
13 Temple of Ishtar
14 Temple of Marduk
15 Temple of Gula
16 Temple of Ninurta
17 Temple of Shamash
18 Temple tower
19 Processional way
20 Palace of Nebuchadnezzar
21 Esagila
22 Northern Citadel
23 Citadel
24 Southern Citadel
25 Outer wall
26 Inner wall
27 Nebuchadnezzar's
   outer wall
28 Canal

This diagram was graciously provided by Lion Publishing Corporation and also appears in a book by Alan Millard titled *Treasures from Bible Times* (Belleville, Mich.: Lion Publishing Corp., 1985). p. 137.

13

II. Facing the Test

The biblical text goes on to say that once Nebuchadnezzar became ruler of Babylonia, he "ordered Ashpenaz, the chief of his officials, to bring in some of the sons of Israel, including some of the royal family and of the nobles" as candidates for the king's service (Dan. 1:3). As we will see, this summons would lead to a test of Daniel's religious convictions.

A. The choice. Ashpenaz had to follow a specific criteria for selecting the right Hebrews for training to become servants of the king. First, the Hebrews were to be "youths" (v. 4a). The Hebrew word translated *youths* refers to teenagers, most likely young people between the ages of thirteen and fifteen. Second, they were to be without "defect"—having no physical or mental handicap (v. 4a). Third, they were to be "good-looking" (v. 4a). Fourth, these Hebrew youths had to manifest "intelligence in every branch of wisdom, [be] endowed with understanding, and [have] discerning knowledge" (v. 4b). And fifth, they had to possess the "ability for serving in the king's court" (v. 4b).

B. The course. Nebuchadnezzar commanded Ashpenaz to put the Hebrew teenagers he would select through a rigorous course of training. This educational program was to last three years and include instruction in "the literature and language of the Chaldeans [i.e., Babylonians]" (vv. 4c, 5b). In other words, the Hebrew youths subjected to this curriculum were to be steeped in Babylonian philosophy, religion, magic, astrology, science, and medicine, to name just a few of the subjects. Moreover, they had to learn this information in the primary language of the Babylonians, "which may originally have been a northeastern Arabian dialect, perhaps mingled with Aramaic," and in the official literary language of Babylonia, which was Akkadian.[5] One obvious goal of this kind of training was to convert the monotheistic Hebrews to Babylonian polytheism. Nebuchadnezzar wanted these Israelites to reject the God they worshiped and the lifestyle they had embraced in Judah and, instead, to serve the false gods of Babylonia and adopt that nation's heathenish lifestyle. Besides reeducating the selected Hebrew teenagers, King Nebuchadnezzar "appointed for them a daily ration from [his] choice food and from the wine which he drank" (v. 5a). Old Testament scholar Gleason Archer observes,

> Probably most of the meat items on the [king's] menu were taken from animals sacrificed to the patron

5. Gleason L. Archer, Jr., "Daniel," in *The Expositor's Bible Commentary,* 12 vols., edited by Frank E. Gaebelein (Grand Rapids, Mich.: Regency Reference Library, Zondervan Publishing House, 1976–   ), vol. 7, p. 34.

gods of Babylon (Marduk, Nebo, and Ishtar, for example), and no doubt the wine from the king's table (v. 5) had first been part of the libation to these deities. Therefore even those portions of food and drink not inherently unclean had been tainted by contact with pagan cultic usage.[6]

Thus, even the food and drink that the Hebrews were to be served had been chosen for the purpose of forcing them to compromise their convictions. As a further measure of indoctrination, the Israelite youths were given Babylonian names. Four of these teenagers—Daniel, Hananiah, Mishael, and Azariah—were renamed after Babylonian deities (vv. 6–7). Daniel was to be called *Belteshazzar*, which may mean either "Lady [wife of Marduk], protect the king," or "Nebo, protect his life." Hananiah was given the name *Shadrach*, meaning either "I am very fearful [of God]" or "the command of Aku [a Sumerian or Elamite moon-god]." Mishael's name was changed to *Meshach*, which means "Who is what God [Aku] is," and Azariah received the name *Abed-nego*, meaning "servant of the Shining One [or of Nego, a Babylonian deity]."[7] Clearly, Daniel and his companions were being faced with a situation that would test their faith in, and obedience to, the God of Scripture.

III. Passing the Test

The remainder of Daniel 1 tells us how the teenager Daniel passed this test of faith without compromising his convictions in the least. Let's see how he did it.

A. Inner conviction. Daniel resolved "that he would not defile himself with the king's choice food or with the wine which he drank" (v. 8a). Apparently, some of the food Daniel was to consume had been declared unclean in the Mosaic Law (Lev. 11, Deut. 14:3–21). It was certainly true that the Law frowned on eating the meat of animals that had been sacrificed to pagan deities (Exod. 34:15, Num. 25:1–2, Deut. 32:37–38). Therefore, Daniel could not have lived on this diet without violating God's Law. Furthermore, according to eastern traditions, " 'to share a meal was to commit oneself to friendship.' " Given this, it may also have been the case that " 'the defilement [Daniel] feared was not so much a ritual as a moral defilement, arising from the subtle flattery of gifts and favours which entailed hidden implications of loyal support.' "[8] In any case, it is clear that

6. Archer, "Daniel," pp. 33–34.

7. Archer, "Daniel," pp. 34–35, and John C. Whitcomb, *Daniel*, Everyman's Bible Commentary (Chicago: Moody Press, 1985), p. 29.

8. Joyce G. Baldwin, *Daniel: An Introduction and Commentary.* Tyndale OT Commentaries. (Downers Grove, Ill.: InterVarsity Press, 1978), p. 83 as quoted in Whitcomb, *Daniel*, pp. 30–31.

Daniel committed himself to remaining pure regardless of the disgrace or danger it could have brought him.

B. Wise approach. Once he had made his decision, Daniel "sought permission from the commander of the officials that he might not defile himself" (Dan. 1:8b). The Hebrew lad acted out of conviction, but he did so with respect for authority—even ungodly authority. However, the Babylonian commander refused to change Daniel's menu. He was afraid that Nebuchadnezzar would kill him if the new diet proved to be less beneficial for the health of Daniel and his companions (v. 10). So young Daniel approached the guard that had been placed in charge of him and his three friends and said,

> "Please test your servants for ten days, and let us be given some vegetables [the Hebrew word also includes grains] to eat and water to drink. Then let our appearance be observed in your presence, and the appearance of the youths who are eating the king's choice food; and deal with your servants according to what you see." (vv. 12–13)

Daniel acted wisely. He went through the proper channels, never treating those over him with contempt. And he believed from the outset that God would honor his faithfulness.

C. Divine assistance. Daniel's trust in the Lord was not in vain. The guard granted Daniel permission to try his proposed diet for ten days (v. 14). At the end of the trial period, Daniel and his friends "seemed better [in appearance] and they were fatter than all the youths who had been eating the king's choice food. So the overseer continued to withhold their choice food and the wine they were to drink, and kept giving them vegetables" (vv. 15–16). God blessed Daniel and his companions for their obedience to Him.

D. Superior standing. As these four Hebrew teenagers remained on their diet and persevered through their studies, "God gave them knowledge and intelligence in every branch of literature and wisdom; Daniel even understood all kinds of visions and dreams" (v. 17). When their instruction was complete, "the commander of the officials presented them before Nebuchadnezzar" (v. 18). After the king talked to them and the other Hebrew trainees, "not one was found like Daniel, Hananiah, Mishael and Azariah; so they entered the king's personal service. And as for every matter of wisdom and understanding about which the king consulted them, he found them ten times better than all the magicians and conjurers who were in all his realm" (vv. 19–20). Daniel and his friends graduated at the top of their class. In fact, God blessed them so abundantly that they even surpassed the understanding of the Babylonian wise men. And of the four, at least Daniel continued to prosper in the Babylonian royal court "until the first year of Cyrus the king" (v. 21)—a Persian monarch who ruled over Babylonia from about 539 to 530 B.C.

IV. Some Lasting Principles

In a world filled with people who rebel against the divine King, it is inevitable that believers of all ages will face situations in which their convictions will be challenged. We who are parents need to prepare our children for those occasions by both teaching them God's truth and modeling integrity. And all of us who are Christians need to personally commit ourselves to living God's way regardless of the temptations to live otherwise. Recalling and applying two principles that are embedded in the first chapter of Daniel will help us keep that commitment.

A. Inner conviction can overcome any outer pressure to compromise.

B. God-honoring convictions yield God-given rewards.

Living Insights

Study One

The story of Daniel and his three friends is an exciting one. It's the account of four adolescents who manifested conviction, wisdom, and honor in their walk with God. Let's get a feel for all twelve chapters of the book that bears Daniel's name.

• Use the following chart to guide your survey of the Book of Daniel. As you read the first six chapters, seek to categorize what you discover under the four headings listed below. Record your findings on a copy of this chart. We will focus on the last six chapters of Daniel in the next Living Insights exercise.

A Survey of Daniel 1–6			
Tests Encountered	Character Traits	Dreams	Interpretations

Continued on next page

17

Living Insights

Critical tests, character traits, dreams, and interpretations make up most of the Book of Daniel. Let's continue our survey of this great narrative.

● In this study let's focus our attention on the last six chapters of Daniel. Complete a copy of the following chart, filling it in with examples of each of the topics listed as headings below.

A Survey of Daniel 7–12			
Tests Encountered	Character Traits	Dreams	Interpretations

A King on the Couch
Daniel 2:1–30

The Bible records numerous means God has used to reveal Himself and His Word to man (Heb. 1:1–2). Two vehicles of revelation He has often utilized are visions and dreams (Num. 12:6). God has used visions to present "certain scenery or circumstances to the mind of a person while awake" (Isa. 6).[1] Many times, however, the Lord has communicated His message to people while they were asleep (Gen. 28:10–17, Matt. 1:19–21). The Babylonian king, Nebuchadnezzar, experienced this, even though he was not a believer in the one true God. However, this polytheistic monarch was not able to interpret his own dream. As we will see, the lives of Daniel and his three Hebrew friends were endangered because of this situation. Even so, they did not panic but turned to God and sought His help. From this ancient story we will learn some principles that can help us handle predicaments which are humanly impossible to solve.

I. The Historical Setting

King Nebuchadnezzar reigned over the Babylonian Empire from 605 to 562 B.C. During the second year of his rule, he had a series of dreams which troubled him so much that he could not sleep (Dan. 2:1). So "the king gave orders to call in the magicians, the conjurers, the sorcerers and the Chaldeans, to tell the king his dreams" (v. 2a). The magicians were diviners who used charts or magical designs to answer people's questions. Conjurers were soothsayers who "uttered spells or potent combinations of words or phrases thought to possess the ability to accomplish desired magical results."[2] The sorcerers practiced the black magic art of contacting the dead to discover the future. And the Chaldeans were "a special class of astrologer-soothsayers" who apparently acted as spokesmen for the other groups of Babylonian wise men that the king had summoned.[3] With these individuals before him, Nebuchadnezzar said, "I had a dream, and my spirit is anxious to understand the dream" (v. 3). He did not tell his dream to these wise men, but expected them to recount and interpret it by drawing on their own magical and spiritual resources. In demanding this, Nebuchadnezzar was assuming that if they were able to discover the content of his dream on their own, they would also be able to interpret it correctly.

1. Merrill F. Unger, "Vision," in *Unger's Bible Dictionary*, 3d ed., rev. (Chicago: Moody Press, 1966), p. 1159.

2. Gleason L. Archer, Jr., "Daniel," in *The Expositor's Bible Commentary*, 12 vols. (Grand Rapids, Mich.: Regency Reference Library, Zondervan Publishing House, 1976–   ), Vol. 7, p. 38.

3. Archer, "Daniel," p. 40.

II. The Failure of the Babylonian Wise Men

In response to the king's request, the Chaldeans said, " 'O king, live forever! Tell the dream to your servants, and we will declare the interpretation' " (v. 4). The Babylonian wise men were trying to get around Nebuchadnezzar's challenge because they knew that they could not meet it. But Nebuchadnezzar would not back down. He told them,

> "The command from me is firm: if you do not make known to me the dream and its interpretation, you will be torn limb from limb, and your houses will be made a rubbish heap. But if you declare the dream and its interpretation, you will receive from me gifts and a reward and great honor; therefore declare to me the dream and its interpretation" (vv. 5–6).

Again, the wise men asked the king to tell them his dream first (v. 7), but Nebuchadnezzar would do no such thing. Detecting the wise men's motives, Nebuchadnezzar retorted,

> "I know for certain that you are bargaining for time, inasmuch as you have seen that the command from me is firm, that if you do not make the dream known to me, there is only one decree for you. For you have agreed together to speak lying and corrupt words before me until the situation is changed; therefore tell me the dream, that I may know that you can declare to me its interpretation." (vv. 8–9)

Now that their inability to discover the king's dream was exposed, the sages defended themselves:

> "There is not a man on earth who could declare the matter for the king, inasmuch as no great king or ruler has ever asked anything like this of any magician, conjurer or Chaldean. Moreover, the thing which the king demands is difficult, and there is no one else who could declare it to the king except gods, whose dwelling place is not with mortal flesh." (vv. 10–11)

This response caused Nebuchadnezzar to become "indignant and very furious, [so he] gave orders to destroy all the wise men of Babylon" (v. 12). The text informs us that his decree was so far-reaching that it included Daniel and his three companions (v. 13).

III. The Wise Response of Daniel

When Daniel was seized, he "replied with discretion and discernment to Arioch," the one charged with the task of carrying out the king's decree of execution (v. 14). Daniel asked Arioch, " 'For what reason is the decree from the king so urgent?' Then Arioch informed Daniel about the matter" (v. 15). Once Daniel knew what the commotion was about, he went to Nebuchadnezzar and asked the monarch to "give him time, in order that he might declare the interpretation to the king" (v. 16). "Then," the text adds, "Daniel went to his house and informed his friends, Hananiah, Mishael and Azariah, about the matter, in order that they might request compassion from the God of heaven concerning this mystery, so that Daniel and his friends might not be destroyed with the rest of the wise men of Babylon" (vv. 17–18). Daniel understood that a humanly impossible situation can only be resolved with divine intervention. So he sought God's help and waited for His response. We are told that during the night the mystery of Nebuchadnezzar's dream was revealed to Daniel through a vision (v. 19a). After receiving the information needed to save himself and his friends, Daniel turned to God, offering Him words of praise and gratitude (vv. 20–23). Although Daniel could have rushed to the king's palace without thanking God for intervening, he chose to first give the Lord the credit He rightly deserved (cf. Heb. 13:15). Then Daniel informed Arioch that he was ready to interpret the king's dream (Dan. 2:24). After hearing this, Arioch rushed "Daniel into the king's presence and spoke to him as follows: 'I have found a man among the exiles from Judah who can make the interpretation known to the king'" (v. 25). By publicly declaring that he had discovered that Daniel could explain the king's dream, Arioch was trying to exalt himself in the sight of Nebuchadnezzar. Daniel chose to ignore Arioch's attempt to get some recognition and instead, directly addressed the king, giving God all the glory. Notice what he said:

"As for the mystery about which the king has inquired, neither wise men, conjurers, magicians, nor diviners are able to declare it to the king. However, there is a God in heaven who reveals mysteries, and He has made known to King Nebuchadnezzar what will take place in the latter days. This was your dream and the visions in your mind while on your bed. As for you, O king, while on your bed your thoughts turned to what would take place in the future; and He who reveals mysteries has made known to you what will take place. But as for me, this mystery has not been revealed to me for any wisdom residing in me more than in any other living man, but for the purpose of making the interpretation known to the king, and that you may understand the thoughts of your mind." (vv. 27–30)

IV. Some Practical Principles for Today

In the next lesson we will learn about the content and interpretation of Nebuchadnezzar's dream. But before we do, we need to reflect on what we have studied in this lesson and consider how to apply its teaching to our lives. Among the many lessons taught in Daniel 2:1–30, three are prominent.

A. God's work is best seen in humanly impossible predicaments. In fact, He will often bring such situations into our lives so that we will realize our need to trust in Him completely.

B. Our most effective source of stability is prayer. And as this story in the Book of Daniel illustrates, great benefit can come to us when we share our prayer requests with others and ask them to pray with us.

C. When God works, there is only room for praise, not pride. The Lord wants and expects us to give Him the credit for what He accomplishes in our lives. As we do, we will find our selfishness diminishing and our godliness increasing.

Living Insights

Study One

Nebuchadnezzar was not the only government official to ever have a dream that he could not understand. Centuries before, in the land of Egypt, Pharaoh also had a perplexing dream . . . and God provided a man to interpret it. This Old Testament saint was Joseph.

● Read Genesis 40–41. Then, based on what you have learned so far about the prophet Daniel, compare and contrast him with Joseph. Do the same with Pharaoh and Nebuchadnezzar and their dreams. This should prove to be an enlightening study of human character and divine providence.

Joseph and Daniel	
Similarities	Differences

Pharaoh and Nebuchadnezzar	
Similarities	Differences

![Living Insights logo]

Living Insights

Study Two

Did you take careful note of Daniel 2:19? "The mystery was revealed to Daniel in a night vision. Then Daniel blessed the God of heaven." This young teenager stopped to praise God for giving him an answer!

- Daniel's praise to God is recorded in Daniel 2:20–23. When was the last time you gave honor to God? Use this opportunity to do that right now. On a clean sheet of paper, write down some honest expressions of praise to God. Center your thoughts on *who He is* and *what He has done* in your life. But beware: This act of worship can lead to positive, lifetime changes in your conduct. It is our hope that this godly medium of gratitude will become addictive!

A Blueprint of Tomorrow
Daniel 2:31–49

In the last lesson we learned that King Nebuchadnezzar had such a distressing dream that he was unable to sleep. He was so troubled by this dream that he assembled the best wise men in Babylon to recount and interpret it for him. When these counselors failed to provide the right answers, Nebuchadnezzar ordered that they, along with all the other wise men of Babylon, be executed. Before the king's command could be carried out, God revealed the content and interpretation of the dream to Daniel. What the Lord communicated to Daniel forms the backbone of biblical prophecy concerning the rise and fall of Gentile kingdoms. Although many of the events set forth in the king's dream have already been fulfilled in history, some are still to occur. We can be confident that those happenings which have not yet taken place will come to pass at the proper time in God's plan. Let's delve into the details of Nebuchadnezzar's dream and take a look at what tomorrow holds.

I. The Revelation of the Dream

When Daniel was brought before Nebuchadnezzar, he gave God the credit for unveiling the mystery that surrounded the king's dream (Dan. 2:25–30; cf. v. 19). Then Daniel proceeded to relay the content of the dream to Nebuchadnezzar. He began by saying,

> "You, O king, were looking and behold, there was a single great statue; that statue, which was large and of extraordinary splendor, was standing in front of you, and its appearance was awesome. The head of that statue was made of fine gold, its breast and its arms of silver, its belly and its thighs of bronze, its legs of iron, its feet partly of iron and partly of clay." (vv. 31–33)

The head of this magnificent statue was composed of the finest material, but from the figure's breast and arms down to its feet, the value of its materials decreased. Furthermore, this statue was to have a limited lifetime. Notice what Daniel said:

> "You continued looking until a stone was cut out without hands, and it struck the statue on its feet of iron and clay, and crushed them. Then the iron [its legs], the clay [its feet], the bronze [its belly and thighs], the silver [its breast and arms] and the gold [its head] were crushed all at the same time, and became like chaff from the summer threshing floors; and the wind carried them away so that not a trace of them was found. But the stone that struck the statue became a great mountain and filled the whole earth." (vv. 34–35)

24

II. The Interpretation of the Dream

After Daniel recounted the dream to Nebuchadnezzar, he gave its interpretation (v. 36). The young Hebrew man explained that the various materials and parts of the statue represented the different Gentile kingdoms that would one day be completely destroyed and replaced by the divine King. Let's observe the details of this prophecy.

A. The Babylonian kingdom. Daniel stated that the head of gold represented the kingdom of Babylonia:

> "You, O king, are the king of kings, to whom the God of heaven has given the kingdom, the power, the strength, and the glory; and wherever the sons of men dwell, or the beasts of the field, or the birds of the sky, He has given them into your hand and has caused you to rule over them all. You are the head of gold." (vv. 37–38)

Nebuchadnezzar must have welled up with pride when he heard those words. But any sense of self-importance he may have experienced was challenged as Daniel continued to interpret the dream.

B. The Medo-Persian kingdom. Daniel said that an inferior kingdom would arise and replace Babylonia (v. 39a). Although this second empire is not named in this verse, it is clear from other passages that the kingdom of silver represented the Medo-Persian Empire (cf. 5:28, 31). Nebuchadnezzar must have wondered how a nation inferior to Babylonia could ever usurp its rule. History, however, yields the answer. Old Testament exegete John C. Whitcomb explains:

> After the death of Nebuchadnezzar in 562 B.C., a drastic deterioration of the qualities of the kingdom occurred under the rule of his son Evil-Merodach, two usurpers of the throne (Neriglissar and Nabonidus), and finally his daughter's son Belshazzar. By 539 B.C. the golden qualities of brilliant and absolute dictatorial autocracy which had characterized the forty-three-year reign of Nebuchadnezzar were almost gone. Then it was that "the time of his own land" finally came, and Cyrus, though inferior to Nebuchadnezzar in the authority by which he ruled (being subject to the laws of the Medes and Persians, 6:8, 15), was nevertheless overwhelmingly greater than the morally rotten Belshazzar, who was weighed in God's balances and found wanting (Dan. 5:27).[1]

1. John C. Whitcomb, *Daniel,* Everyman's Bible Commentary (Chicago: Moody Press, 1985), p. 45.

C. The Grecian kingdom. Following the Medo-Persian Empire would be a third government represented by bronze. Daniel prophesied that this kingdom would " 'rule over all the earth' " (2:39b). The political power he was referring to was the Grecian Empire (cf. 8:21). Beginning in 334 B.C., under the military leadership of Alexander the Great, Greece conquered Medo-Persia and all the regions to the east, as far as the borders of India. From Daniel's perspective, it seemed that all the known world would fall under the dominion of Greece. Although the Greeks did become a great power because of their military strength, they lacked administrative efficiency. In that sense, at least, they were inferior to their predecessors.

D. The Roman kingdom. The fourth kingdom to come onto the stage of human history would be " 'as strong as iron; inasmuch as iron crushes and shatters all things, so, like iron that breaks in pieces, it will crush and break all these in pieces' " (2:40). The Roman Empire's war machine slowly but completely rolled over the lands that had composed the other three kingdoms, assimilating their people and their cultures under one government. However, the Roman kingdom would never successfully unite all the peoples it ruled. Daniel said that it would be a " 'divided kingdom,' " and one that would be partially strong and partially brittle (vv. 41–42). In A.D. 395, the western and eastern divisions of the Roman Empire became firmly established. And throughout its one-thousand-year existence, the kingdom of Rome suffered internal strife and moral decay. But even after the last Roman emperor of the West was deposed by the Goths in A.D. 476, the iron-like strengths of Roman rule continued. The Middle Ages that followed could not remove what proved to be an indelible imprint of Roman culture. In fact, the barbarians that conquered Rome accepted and adapted many of the empire's central elements, including its view of law. Even Roman Catholicism was instrumental in preserving and spreading Romanism throughout Eruope and into the New World.[2] In short, though the Roman Empire as a political entity is long since dead, many of its institutions and ideals still live on in the nations of the West. Indeed, just as Rome tried to unite imperialism—the iron-like will of authority—and democracy— the clay-like voice of the populace—so the Western world has also made its attempts to do so. However, just as Rome was unable to combine them (v. 43), so the countries of the West

2. See "Rome," in *The Columbia Encyclopedia,* 3d ed. (New York: Columbia University, 1963).

will never fully succeed in uniting governmental authority and democratic ideals.

E. The divine Kingdom. The stone that was not made by human hands " 'will crush and put an end to all these kingdoms' " (v. 44b). As John C. Whitcomb explains, the prophecy concerning the destruction of the entire statue by this stone "is historically, culturally, and religiously accurate."[3]

> Just as the silver kingdom absorbed Neo-Babylonian religion and culture into itself . . . , so also Alexander the Great adapted Greek culture to Persian culture, which resulted in a new Hellenistic amalgam. And finally, Rome did not annihilate the religious, philosophic, and cultural aspects of the various Greek and Hellenistic kingdoms but incorporated them into the multifaceted empire called Rome [which is still influential today].[4]

When Jesus Christ returns to earth to establish His Millennial Kingdom, He will " 'break [the nations] with a rod of iron, / [He will] shatter them like earthenware' " (Ps. 2:9). As the smitting stone in Nebuchadnezzar's dream, the Lord will not absorb, restructure, or adapt to previous kingdoms; He will totally annihilate them and set up His own monarchy, which will be absolutely perfect politically, morally, economically, and religiously. And He will rule over all the earth as King of kings and Lord of lords (Isa. 2:2–4; cf. Rev. 19:11–16).

III. The Promotion of the Prophet

After Daniel gave the interpretation of the dream, "King Nebuchadnezzar fell on his face and did homage to Daniel, and gave orders to present to him an offering and fragrant incense" (Dan. 2:46). The king also told Daniel, " 'Surely your God is a God of gods and a Lord of kings and a revealer of mysteries, since you have been able to reveal this mystery' " (v. 47). This confession was quite remarkable, given the fact that Nebuchadnezzar was a polytheist. The text adds that "the king promoted Daniel and gave him many great gifts, and he made him ruler over the whole province of Babylon and chief prefect over all the wise men of Babylon" (v. 48). Daniel, however, desired to serve with his three friends, who were also his prayer partners. So "Daniel made request of the king, and he appointed Shadrach, Meshach and Abed-nego over the administration of the province of Babylon, while Daniel was at the king's court" (v. 49).

---

3. Whitcomb, *Daniel,* p. 47.

4. Whitcomb, *Daniel,* p. 47.

IV. Some Truths Drawn from the Message

Although no one but God knows specifically when Christ will come back as the earth's Ruler (Matt. 24:36–37, Acts 1:6–7), we can be sure of at least two things regarding His return.

A. We are rapidly approaching the end of human rule as we know it. After all, we have been in the "last days" since Christ's Ascension nearly two thousand years ago (Acts 2:14–17, 2 Tim. 3:1–5, Heb. 1:1–2). That puts us two thousand years closer to the moment of His return.

B. All investments in earthly kingdoms are temporary at best. Therefore, we should invest our efforts in seeking and spreading God's heavenly kingdom on earth (Matt. 5:13–16, 6:19–21, 25–33; John 4:27–38). This involves trusting in Christ as our Savior and serving Him as our Lord. Will you commit yourself to doing these things today? Tomorrow may be too late.

 Living Insights

Study One ▬▬▬▬▬▬▬▬▬▬▬▬▬▬▬▬▬▬▬▬▬▬▬▬▬

Daniel 2 is one of the most intriguing chapters in the entire Word of God. There is so much to grasp in these forty-nine verses. Let's take a more personal approach to this passage.

• Can you sense the emotion behind the words of Daniel 2? One way to get in touch with those feelings is through the discipline of *paraphrasing.* Write out Daniel 2:1–49 in your own words. Use this as an opportunity to bring out the thoughts and feelings that undoubtedly undergird the text. If forty-nine verses seem to be too much, try a smaller portion, such as verses 1–24 or 31–49. Don't miss out on this chance to personally interact with the Scriptures.

Living Insights

Study Two ▬▬▬▬▬▬▬▬▬▬▬▬▬▬▬▬▬▬▬▬▬▬▬▬▬

The last verse of Daniel 2 makes us smile. Nebuchadnezzar promoted Daniel in the preceding verse, and, in verse 49, Daniel shares the blessing with his friends. But these young men were more than friends; they were Daniel's prayer partners (vv. 17–18a).

• Do you have a prayer partner? Is there a person in your life that shares the burdens of your requests and feels the joy when you receive answers? If you do, give that person a call or write them a note expressing your appreciation. If you don't have a prayer partner, take steps to find one. Look for someone who will respect you and allow you to be vulnerable. The time you spend seeking out this individual and cultivating the relationship with him or her will be time well spent.

A Ragtime Band
and a Fiery Furnace
Daniel 3, 1 Peter 2:18–20

Have you ever been told, "Once you become a Christian, you will have it made; your problems will disappear, and your life will be pure joy"? Or, "If you do what is right, you will never experience ill-treatment"? Neither of these statements is supported in Scripture. In fact, the Bible affirms repeatedly that Christians will suffer unjustly. Notice what the Apostle Peter says:

> Servants, be submissive to your masters with all respect, not only to those who are good and gentle, but also to those who are unreasonable. For this finds favor, if for the sake of conscience toward God a man bears up under sorrows when suffering unjustly. For what credit is there if, when you sin and are harshly treated, you endure it with patience? But if when you do what is right and suffer for it you patiently endure it, this finds favor with God. (1 Pet. 2:18–20)

Some Old Testament believers who modeled this New Testament teaching are presented in the third chapter of Daniel. Here we learn about three Jews who faced a horrible death simply because they obeyed God. The truths we will discover from this ancient yet familiar story can help us handle the tough circumstances and unfair treatment that will inevitably come our way.

I. The King's Image

The first twelve verses of Daniel 3 set the stage for a life-and-death test to be given to Shadrach, Meshach, and Abed-nego—the prophet Daniel's three Hebrew friends. Let's take a close look at these verses.

A. Construction. The text informs us that "Nebuchadnezzar the king made an image of gold, the height of which was sixty cubits [90 feet] and its width six cubits [9 feet]; he set it up on the plain of Dura in the province of Babylon" (Dan. 3:1). There are several observations we should make concerning this verse. First, we are not told when Nebuchadnezzar built this monument. We may conclude, however, that a sufficient amount of time had elapsed in order for the Babylonian ruler to have forgotten what he had learned about God during the events described in Daniel 2. The Septuagint, a Greek version of the Hebrew Old Testament, adds that Nebuchadnezzar constructed this image in the eighteenth year of his reign—approximately sixteen years after his dream had been interpreted by the prophet Daniel (2:2). If the Septuagint is correct, this statue was erected around 586 B.C.—the year Nebuchadnezzar destroyed

30

Jerusalem and thereby presumably defeated and discredited the God of Israel. Such a victory provided an excellent opportunity for the polytheist Nebuchadnezzar to erect an image designed to help unify his empire and consolidate his authority. Second, we are not told what or whom the statue represented. However, Old Testament exegete Gleason Archer reasons that it is doubtful the image was of the king, for "we have no evidence that statues of a Mesopotamian ruler were ever worshiped as divine during the ruler's lifetime. . . . [Therefore], it is far more likely that the statue represented Nebuchadnezzar's patron God, Nebo (or Nabu). Prostration before Nebo would amount to a pledge of allegiance to his viceroy, . . . Nebuchadnezzar."[1] Third, the statue must have been overlaid in gold, since there was not enough of this precious metal in all Babylonia to make such a large monument of solid gold. Fourth, the all-gold appearance of this monument suggests that Nebuchadnezzar had come to believe that his kingdom would last forever, not be overthrown by an inferior power as Daniel had prophesied (v. 39a). Fifth, because this eight-story-high statue was erected on a plain near the capital of Babylonia, it must have been an impressive sight for the Babylon populace to behold and readily accessible to the government officials that lived and worked there.

B. Dedication. After the image was constructed and erected, "Nebuchadnezzar the king sent word to assemble the satraps [governors of large provinces], the prefects [possibly military commanders, but more likely lieutenant governors] and the governors [administrators of small territories], the counselors [advisors to government officials], the treasurers [administrators of the government's funds], the judges [administrators of the laws of Babylonia], the magistrates [enforcers of the law] and all the rulers of the provinces [governmental executives] to come to the dedication of the image." (3:2)[2]

Once these state authorities were assembled "before the image that Nebuchadnezzar had set up" (v. 3), the king's herald proclaimed this message:

"To you the command is given, O peoples, nations and men of every language, that at the moment you hear

1. Gleason L. Archer, Jr., "Daniel," in *The Expositor's Bible Commentary,* 12 vols., edited by Frank E. Gaebelein (Grand Rapids, Mich.: Regency Reference Library, Zondervan Publishing House, 1976–   ), vol. 7, pp. 50–51.

2. See Archer, "Daniel," p. 51, and J. Dwight Pentecost, "Daniel," in *The Bible Knowledge Commentary: Old Testament Edition,* edited by John F. Walvoord and Roy B. Zuck (Wheaton, Ill.: Victor Books, 1985), p. 1338.

the sound of the horn, flute, lyre, trigon, psaltery, bagpipe, and all kinds of music, you are to fall down and worship the golden image that Nebuchadnezzar the king has set up. But whoever does not fall down and worship shall immediately be cast into the midst of a furnace of blazing fire." (vv. 4–6)

Confronted by the king's command and probably within earshot of the roaring furnace, the governmental authorities bowed down and paid homage to the statue when the orchestra began to play (v. 7). Their adherence to the royal edict signified the submission of the people they represented to Nebuchadnezzar's political and religious authority. However, when the throng of government leaders touched their foreheads to the ground in worship, three Hebrews remained standing.

C. Accusation. Because they refused to heed the king's edict, charges were brought against them by some of the Chaldeans. These Babylonians came before the king and said in part: " 'There are certain Jews whom you have appointed over the administration of the province of Babylon, namely Shadrach, Meshach and Abed-nego. These men, O king, have disregarded you; they do not serve your gods or worship the golden image which you have set up' " (v. 12). No doubt, Daniel would have been named here if he had been present at the dedication of the statue.[3] For he certainly would have joined his friends in defying Nebuchadnezzar's command, since to do otherwise would have placed him at odds with God's command not to worship false gods (Deut. 5:8–10). And Daniel had already demonstrated his faithfulness to the God of Israel early in his dealings with the Babylonian government. Although Daniel was spared being accused of treason, his longtime companions were not. Indeed, they were about to face the test of their lives.

II. The Fiery Furnace

Even though Shadrach, Meshach, and Abed-nego had done what was right as far as God was concerned, they had committed an abominable act of rebellion in the eyes of Nebuchadnezzar.[4]

---

3. Archer deals with this issue quite thoroughly in his commentary titled "Daniel," p. 55.

4. Shadrach, Meshach, and Abed-nego were faced with an ethical dilemma: obey God's command to submit to human government, or obey the divine injunction to worship only the Lord. These Hebrews chose to follow the latter command rather than the former, and God honored their decision by delivering them from physical death. This incident raises a host of ethical questions that Christians have answered in various ways. For more information on the issues involved and the positions Christians have taken, see the study guides titled *Moses: God's Man for a Crisis* (edited by Bill Watkins, from the Bible-teaching ministry of Charles R. Swindoll [Fullerton, Calif.: Insight for Living, 1985]), pp. 6–7, and *Relating to Others in Love: A Study of Romans 12–16* (edited by Bill Watkins, from the Bible-teaching ministry of Charles R. Swindoll [Fullerton, Calif.: Insight for Living, 1985]), pp. 17–24.

A. The king's outrage. "In rage and anger," the Babylonian monarch ordered that the Jewish offenders be brought to him (Dan. 3:13). After questioning them about their noncompliance, he gave them one more chance " 'to fall down and worship the image' " at the sound of the music (vv. 14–15a). If they refused this time, they would " 'immediately be cast into the midst of a furnace of blazing fire' " (v. 15b). To these words Nebuchadnezzar added, " 'And what god is there who can deliver you out of my hands?' " (v. 15c).

B. The Hebrews' faith. Shadrach, Meshach, and Abed-nego did not waver in their loyalty to God. They told the king,

> "O Nebuchadnezzar, we do not need to give you an answer concerning this. If it be so, our God whom we serve is able to deliver us from the furnace of blazing fire; and He will deliver us out of your hand, O king. But even if He does not, let it be known to you, O king, that we are not going to serve your gods or worship the golden image that you have set up." (vv. 16–18)

C. The furnace's intensity. The response of these three Jews was intolerable to the king. In his rage, Nebuchadnezzar went to absurd lengths to guarantee their execution. Although no human being could have survived an instant in the fiery furnace, the king ordered "that additional bellows be inserted under the blazing coals and that it be heated to maximum intensity"[5] (v. 19b). Then he insisted that the three offenders be bound fully clothed, as if the clothing could have caused them to be consumed more quickly than they would have been without it (vv. 20–21). When these Jews were thrown into the raging furnace, those who tossed them in were killed by the intense heat (vv. 22–23). For the moment it looked as if Shadrach, Meshach, and Abed-nego had breathed their last.

D. The Lord's deliverance. What happened next astounded Nebuchadnezzar and brought him hastily to his feet (v. 24a). Addressing his high officials, the king said, " 'Was it not three men we cast bound into the midst of the fire?' They answered and said to the king, 'Certainly' " (v. 24b). Then Nebuchadnezzar responded, " 'Look! I see four men loosed and walking about in the midst of the fire without harm, and the appearance of the fourth is like a son of the gods!' " (v. 25). The king could not believe what he saw. Not only were the Hebrews still alive, but they were free and moving about with someone who had the appearance of deity. Coming as close to the furnace as he

---

5. Archer, "Daniel," p. 56.

possibly could, Nebuchadnezzar called the three Hebrews to come out (v. 26a). After they emerged from the flames, they were inspected by all the government officials that had witnessed the miracle (vv. 26b–27). The Babylonians discovered that the bodies and clothes of the Jews showed no signs of being burned by the incredible fire. The Hebrews did not even smell of fire (v. 27). The only thing that had been destroyed in the furnace were their bonds. God had sovereignly chosen to deliver them from the flames and to demonstrate His authority over King Nebuchadnezzar.

E. The king's response. In humility, Nebuchadnezzar spoke: "Blessed be the God of Shadrach, Meshach and Abednego, who has sent His angel and delivered His servants who put their trust in Him, violating the king's command, and yielded up their bodies so as not to serve or worship any god except their own God. Therefore, I make a decree that any people, nation or tongue that speaks anything offensive against the God of Shadrach, Meshach and Abednego shall be torn limb from limb and their houses reduced to a rubbish heap, inasmuch as there is no other god who is able to deliver in this way." (vv. 28–29)

"Then," the text adds, Nebuchadnezzar "caused Shadrach, Meshach and Abed-nego to prosper in the province of Babylon" (v. 30).

III. Some Lessons Taught

We can learn many lessons from this ancient account of courage and faith. However, let's concentrate especially on three.

A. God is sovereign, whether the result of our obedience is triumph or tragedy. Shadrach, Meshach, and Abed-nego believed that God was in control of their situation, regardless of whether or not He chose to deliver them from the fire (vv. 17–18). The Lord does not promise that He will spare us from all struggles or save us from all difficulties. However, He does assure us that He will bring good out of everything, even though every occurrence is not good or right in itself (Rom. 8:28; cf. the Book of Job).

B. Suffering is necessary, whether it seems fair or not. The three Jewish believers were persecuted for doing what was right. Situations like this may not be fair, but they can be used for our good. Just as the Lord used the fire in Nebuchadnezzar's furnace to burn away the cords that bound the Hebrews, so He employs the heat of adversity and trial to remove sin from our lives and transform us into Christ's likeness (James 1:2–4, Rom. 8:28–30).

C. Deliverance is impressive, whether it is witnessed by the godly or the ungodly. Shadrach, Meshach, and Abed-nego could never have impacted Nebuchadnezzar's life so powerfully if they had not been mistreated by this king and delivered by God. As a result of their furnace experience, Nebuchadnezzar's interest in, and respect for, the God of Israel was renewed and heightened. The Lord can do the same through us if we respond to tribulations with an attitude of trust in Him, regardless of the possible outcome.

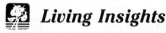 *Living Insights*

Study One ▬▬▬▬▬▬▬▬▬▬▬▬▬▬▬▬▬▬▬▬▬▬▬▬

The account of Shadrach, Meshach, and Abed-nego in the fiery furnace is familiar to many people. Did you notice the musical instruments mentioned in the story? They play an important role in the unfolding of this incredible event. Let's do some background study on the instruments used in Nebuchadnezzar's orchestra.

● Copy the following chart into your notebook. Then turn to Daniel 3:5 and list the musical instruments named there. Find a Bible dictionary—such as *Unger's Bible Dictionary,* by Merrill F. Unger—and look up the instruments you have noted. In Unger's dictionary the various instruments are discussed under the heading "Music." Then, in the right-hand column, summarize the information you discovered about each instrument.

Musical Instruments Used in Babylon—Daniel 3:5	
Instruments	Descriptions

🌳 *Living Insights*

Many twentieth-century Christians are in a fiery furnace that God has sovereignly allowed for their good. This fact is worth pondering.

- On a page of your notebook record your thoughts about the fiery furnace in your life. Express your feelings with total candor. Are you experiencing any bitterness because of this situation? Use this activity as a time of confession and cleansing, or as an opportunity to remind yourself of God's purpose for trials.

My Fiery Furnace

What it is:

How I've dealt with it in the past:

How I'll be dealing with it from now on:

What God is teaching me through this experience:

Insomnia, Insanity, and Insight
Daniel 4

The fourth chapter of Daniel is one of the most intriguing portions of the Bible. Much of it is a monologue by King Nebuchadnezzar. We discover in verse 1 that this chapter is a proclamation from Nebuchadnezzar to the people under Babylonian rule. Many Bible scholars suggest that the prophet Daniel may have helped the king prepare this declaration.[1] Even if this is true, however, the fourth chapter of Daniel is the only passage in all of Scripture that was probably composed under the authority of a new believer. As we will see, there is evidence in the Book of Daniel that this polytheistic ruler became converted in mind and heart to Jewish monotheism, and thereby experienced salvation. But if Nebuchadnezzar was not saved as a result of the events recorded in Daniel 4, he at least came to intellectually accept and politically submit to the one true God. In either case, this passage of Scripture relays an incredible story about the Lord's sovereignty and the extent to which He will go to demonstrate His authority.

I. The King and His Dream

Chapter 4 contains the words of a nation-wide address: "Nebuchadnezzar the king to all the peoples, nations, and men of every language that live in all the earth: 'May your peace abound!' " The date this proclamation was issued is uncertain. However, many Bible scholars believe that it was given late in Nebuchadnezzar's reign (605–562 B.C.), probably between 575 and 563.[2] This would indicate that the events described in his declaration occurred during an eight-year span sometime between 583 and 563.

A. A declaration of purpose and praise. In Daniel 4:2, Nebuchadnezzar explains why he has chosen to make this announcement. " 'It has seemed good to me to declare the signs and wonders which the Most High God has done for me.' " Then Nebuchadnezzar goes on to exalt the Lord with words of praise:

"How great are His signs,
And how mighty are His wonders!
His kingdom is an everlasting kingdom,
And His dominion is from generation to
generation." (v. 3)

---

1. John C. Whitcomb, *Daniel,* Everyman's Bible Commentary (Chicago: Moody Press, 1985), p. 62; Gleason L. Archer, Jr., "Daniel," in *The Expositor's Bible Commentary,* 12 vols., edited by Frank E. Gaebelein (Grand Rapids, Mich.: Regency Reference Library, Zondervan Publishing House, 1976–   ), vol. 7, p. 58; John F. Walvoord, *Daniel: The Key to Prophetic Revelation* (Chicago: Moody Press, 1971), p. 98.

2. Archer, "Daniel," pp. 59–60; Whitcomb, *Daniel,* pp. 62–63; J. Dwight Pentecost, "Daniel," in *The Bible Knowledge Commentary: Old Testament Edition,* edited by John F. Walvoord and Roy B. Zuck (Wheaton, Ill.: Victor Books, 1985), p. 1341.

What happened in this monarch's life to bring about such a radical change in perspective? After all, he had been worshiping the gods of Babylonia, but now he is uplifting the God of Israel as the Deity above all deities. Nebuchadnezzar tells us in the rest of his proclamation what led to the change in his world view.

B. The description of his dream. While lounging comfortably in his luxurious palace, Nebuchadnezzar fell asleep and had another terrifying dream (vv. 4–5). Unable to sleep any longer, he commanded that all the wise men of Babylon be brought before him so that they could interpret his nightmare (v. 6). But these men failed to give the meaning of his dream just as they had several years before (v. 7; cf. 2:1–13). So Nebuchadnezzar turned once more to Daniel (4:8). However, he did so, not because he had faith in Daniel's God, but because he thought Daniel to be especially in tune with the gods of Babylon (vv. 8–9). With the Hebrew seer before him, Nebuchadnezzar described is dream:

" 'I was looking, and behold, there was a tree in the
midst of the earth, and its height was great.
'The tree grew large and became strong,
And its height reached to the sky,
And it was visible to the end of the
whole earth.
Its foliage was beautiful and its
fruit abundant,
And in it was food for all.
The beasts of the field found shade under it,
And the birds of the sky dwelt in its branches,
And all living creatures fed themselves
from it.
'I was looking in the visions in my mind as I lay on
my bed, and behold, an angelic watcher, a holy one,
descended from heaven.
'He shouted out and spoke as follows:
"Chop down the tree and cut off its branches,
Strip off its foliage and scatter its fruit;
Let the beasts flee from under it,
And the birds from its branches.
Yet leave the stump with its roots in
the ground,
But with a band of iron and bronze around it
In the new grass of the field;
And let him be drenched with the dew
of heaven,
And let him share with the beasts in the
grass of the earth.

Let his mind be changed from that of a man,
And let a beast's mind be given to him,
And let seven periods of time pass over him.
This sentence is by the decree of the
     angelic watchers,
And the decision is a command of the
     holy ones,
In order that the living may know
That the Most High is ruler over the realm
     of mankind,
And bestows it on whom He wishes,
And sets over it the lowliest of men." ' "
(vv. 10b–17)

II. The Prophet and His Interpretation

Daniel was stunned when he heard the king recount his dream
(v. 19a). After Nebuchadnezzar tried to console him (v. 19b), Daniel
told the ruler, " ' "My lord, if only the dream applied to those who
hate you, and its interpretation to your adversaries!" ' " (v. 19c).
Because Daniel had become a loyal servant of Nebuchadnezzar, he
wished that he could give the king an interpretation which would
please him. However, Daniel realized that Nebuchadnezzar wanted
to know the true meaning of the dream, so he proceeded to convey
it to him.

A. The dream's explanation. Daniel first pointed out that the
tree in the dream represented Nebuchadnezzar (vv. 20–22). Then
he explained that the destruction of the tree and the transfor-
mation of the stump into an irrational beast depicted what would
happen in Nebuchadnezzar's future. Notice what Daniel said:
     " 'You [will] be driven away from mankind, and your
     dwelling place [will] be with the beasts of the field,
     and you [will] be given grass to eat like cattle and
     be drenched with the dew of heaven; and seven
     periods of time will pass over you, until you recog-
     nize that the Most High is ruler over the realm of
     mankind, and bestows it on whomever He wishes. And
     in that it was commanded to leave the stump with the
     roots of the tree, your kingdom will be assured to you
     after you recognize that it is Heaven that rules.' "
     (vv. 25–26)

B. The prophet's confrontation. After Daniel finished inter-
preting the king's dream, he lovingly and courageously exhorted
Nebuchadnezzar to change his ways so that the discipline
prophesied might be deferred (v. 27).

> ### A Note on Confrontation
> One of the missing ingredients in home and church life today is compassionate confrontation. For one reason or another, we are often either reluctant to confront others with the truth or eager to cut them down to size with any tool at our disposal. The Lord exhorts us to speak the truth in love (Eph. 4:15, 25) and to seek to restore fellow believers "in a spirit of gentleness" (Gal. 6:1a). When we fail to carry out these commands, we not only disobey God but also hurt those whom we love. If we really care for others, whether they be family members, fellow Christians, or work associates, we will express our concern through loving confrontation when necessary.[3]

III. The Lord and His Discipline

The biblical text does not say whether or not King Nebuchadnezzar heeded Daniel's plea. However, the fact that the events described in the dream did not occur until a year later may indicate that Nebuchadnezzar did make an attempt to amend his ways. On the other hand, the twelve-month delay may have been due solely to God's grace and not to any change on the Babylonian king's part. Whatever the case, Nebuchadnezzar experienced the fulfillment of his dream one year after he had learned its interpretation (Dan. 4:29–33). While " 'walking on the roof of the royal palace of Babylon,' " King Nebuchadnezzar " 'reflected and said, "Is this not Babylon the great, which I myself have built as a royal residence by the might of my power and for the glory of my majesty?" ' " (vv. 29b–30). This monarch refused to acknowledge his indebtedness to God, choosing to exalt himself instead. Because of his prideful spirit, Nebuchadnezzar came under the discipline of God:

"While the word was in the king's mouth, a voice came from heaven, saying, 'King Nebuchadnezzar, to you it is declared: sovereignty has been removed from you, and you will be driven away from mankind, and your dwelling place will be with the beasts of the field. You will be given grass to eat like cattle, and seven periods of time will pass over you, until you recognize that the Most High is ruler over the realm of mankind, and bestows it on whomever He wishes.' Immediately the word concerning Nebuchadnezzar was fulfilled; and he was driven away

---

3. Some materials that provide helpful discussions on confronting others in love are these: David Augsburger, *Caring Enough to Confront,* rev. ed. (Ventura, Calif.: Regal Books, 1980); David Augsburger, *When Caring Is Not Enough: Resolving Conflicts through Fair Fighting* (Ventura, Calif.: Regal Books, 1983); Joyce Huggett, *Creative Conflict: How to Confront and Stay Friends* (Downers Grove, Ill.: InterVarsity Press, 1984).

from mankind and began eating grass like cattle, and his body was drenched with the dew of heaven, until his hair had grown like eagles' feathers and his nails like birds' claws." (vv. 31–33)

IV. The King and His Restoration

After seven years of causing Nebuchadnezzar to live like a crazed beast, the Lord restored the king's ability to reason (v. 34a). In this healed state, the humiliated monarch realized what had happened to him and recalled Daniel's prediction and warning. Then, without any hint of resentment toward God, Nebuchadnezzar praised the Lord:

"I blessed the Most High and praised and honored Him
who lives forever;

For His dominion is an everlasting dominion,
And His kingdom endures from generation
to generation.
And all the inhabitants of the earth are accounted
as nothing,
But He does according to His will in the host
of heaven
And among the inhabitants of earth;
And no one can ward off His hand
Or say to Him, 'What hast Thou done?' "
(vv. 34b–35)

God graciously returned Nebuchadnezzar to his former position of authority and even multiplied his greatness beyond what it had been before his lapse into insanity (v. 36). After describing these events, Nebuchadnezzar closed his decree with words of adoration and insight: " 'Now I Nebuchadnezzar praise, exalt, and honor the King of heaven, for all His works are true and His ways just, and He is able to humble those who walk in pride' " (v. 37). These are hardly the comments of an unsaved man. As Bible expositor John F. Walvoord states:

In Daniel 4 Nebuchadnezzar reaches a new spiritual perspicacity. Prior to his experience of insanity, his confessions were those of a pagan whose polytheism permitted the addition of new gods, as illustrated in Daniel 2:47 and 3:28–29. Now Nebuchadnezzar apparently worships the King of heaven only. For this reason, his autobiography is truly remarkable and reflects the fruitfulness of Daniel's influence upon him and probably of Daniel's daily prayers for him. Certainly God is no respecter of persons and can save the high and mighty in this world as well as the lowly.[4]

4. Walvoord, *Daniel,* p. 112.

V. The Account and Its Application

There are at least two truths in Daniel 4 that we should ponder and apply to our lives.

A. God's judgment may be slow, but it is certain. We tend to think that because divine discipline does not often immediately follow our sinful acts, it will never come (cf. Eccles. 8:11). But nothing could be further from the truth! The Bible affirms that God does discipline His people because of His great love for them (Heb. 12:5–10). And although His corrective work in our lives may appear to come slowly on occasion, it will always come at the proper time and in the best way.

B. God will go to great lengths to show us that He is Lord. He will not allow our pride to go unchecked. He will use even intense pain or hardship to remove ingratitude and egotism from our lives so that we will acknowledge our dependence on Him.

Living Insights

Study One ▬▬▬▬▬▬▬▬▬▬▬▬▬▬▬▬▬▬▬▬▬▬▬

As we move quickly through the Book of Daniel, it would be helpful for us to stop occasionally and catch our breath! Daniel 4 is a good place to slow down the pace. Let's examine this chapter in detail.

• Read through Daniel 4:1–37, circling the words you consider to be key in understanding the text. Then make a copy of the following chart in your notebook, and write the terms you circled in the left column. Next, attempt to define the words from the verses in which they appear. If this proves to be too difficult for some of the terms, check other passages where they are used, or a Bible dictionary or commentary. Finally, in the right column state why each word is significant to Daniel 4 as a whole.

Daniel 4:1–37		
Key Words	Definitions	Significance

Living Insights

God's judgment may sometimes be slow, but it is always certain. We tend to forget this fact. When God does not discipline us immediately, we think He never will. But one message of this lesson is clear: We need to be careful not to misinterpret God's silence.

- Ecclesiastes 8:11 is an excellent verse regarding God's timetable:

> Because the sentence against an evil deed is not executed quickly, therefore the hearts of the sons of men among them are given fully to do evil.

This verse drives home a truth worth remembering. Take a few minutes to memorize it. Say it over and over, and allow its truth to penetrate your heart.

The Handwriting on the Wall
Daniel 5

After the death of Nebuchadnezzar in 562 B.C., the Babylonian Empire began to deteriorate. The spiritual lessons Nebuchadnezzar had learned while king were generally not heeded by the monarchs that followed him. Consequently, the stage was set for Babylonia to be conquered by an inferior nation, just as Daniel had predicted many years before (Dan. 2:39a). The fifth chapter of the Book of Daniel records the fall of Babylon and the death of the last Babylonian king, Belshazzar. We will discover that the Babylonians' pride and arrogance led to the defeat of their mighty kingdom and its seemingly impregnable capital. We will also find that this ancient story has some important lessons to teach us about the justice and sovereignty of God and the power of a godly life.

I. A Setting to Understand

Before we turn our attention to Belshazzar and what led to his demise, let's glean some background information that will help us better appreciate the biblical record of these events.

A. The Babylonian monarchs. After King Nebuchadnezzar died in 562 B.C., his son, Evil-Merodach, ruled over Babylonia for two years (562–560). While in power, Evil-Merodach released the captive Jewish ruler Jehoiachin from prison and gave him a place of honor in the Babylonian royal court (2 Kings 25:27–30). In August 560, King Evil-Merodach was assassinated by General Neriglissar, who was this monarch's own brother-in-law and Nebuchadnezzar's son-in-law. Neriglissar ruled for four years (560–556) and was succeeded by his son Labashi-Marduk in 556. Labashi-Marduk was murdered after reigning only nine months. Nabonidus, the leader of the fatal revolt, ruled Babylonia from 556–539. Concerning Nabonidus, Gleason Archer writes:

> He does not seem to have been related to the royal house by blood but apparently married a daughter of Nebuchadnezzar in order to legitimize his seizure of the throne....A devoted worshiper of the moon-god, Sin..., he was the son of a high priestess belonging to his cult.... For commercial and military advantage, he devoted much attention to North Arabia and Edom, which he conquered in 552. During the last ten years of his life, he seems to have spent most of his time in Teima, an important Edomite or North Arabian capital..., and left the central administration to the charge of his son Belshazzar in Babylon itself—

the situation still obtaining during this final year of the [Babylonian] Empire, 539 B.C.[1]

B. The Medo-Persian military. Toward the end of the co-regency of Nabonidus and Belshazzar, the Medo-Persian military, led by Cyrus, marched toward Babylon. This army was met by Nabonidus and the Babylonian troops at Opis, which was on the Tigris River north of Babylon. Belshazzar was left in charge of the defense of Babylon. When Nabonidus suffered significant reversals in his fight with Cyrus, he retreated south toward Teima, leaving the Medo-Persian army free access to the Babylonian capital. This defeat, however, was not taken as a genuine threat by Belshazzar and the inhabitants of Babylon. They had enough stored provisions to see them through several years of siege. Besides, the magnificent fortifications protecting Babylon made the city virtually unassailable. The capital covered more than three thousand acres. It was surrounded by a large moat and by a double wall that was eighty-five feet thick and almost three hundred and fifty feet high. As if this were not enough, an estimated one hundred towers built along this wall provided the Babylonian military all the advantage it needed to ward off an attack against the city.[2] It seemed as if the Medo-Persians had won a hollow victory. Little did Belshazzar realize, however, that despite Babylon's fortifications, his rule was about to come to an end.

II. A Feast to Remember

Apparently unmoved by Cyrus's victory over Nabonidus, "Belshazzar the king held a great feast for a thousand of his nobles, and he was drinking wine in the presence of the thousand" (Dan. 5:1). When the time came for "offering toasts and pouring out libations to the gods of Babylon,"[3] Belshazzar commanded that "the gold and silver vessels which Nebuchadnezzar his [grandfather] had taken out of the temple which was in Jerusalem" be brought out and used for drinking purposes (v. 2). By using these sacred vessels in this way, Belshazzar was defaming the Lord of Israel and exalting himself above the King of kings. The Babylonian ruler's nobles, wives, and concubines joined him in his ridicule of God by drinking wine from

1. Gleason L. Archer, Jr., "Daniel," in *The Expositor's Bible Commentary,* 12 vols., edited by Frank E. Gaebelein (Grand Rapids, Mich.: Regency Reference Library, Zondervan Publishing House, 1976–   ), vol. 7, p. 69. See also John C. Whitcomb, *Daniel,* Everyman's Bible Commentary (Chicago: Moody Press, 1985), pp. 70–73.

2. Archer, "Daniel," p. 69; Howard F. Vos, *Archaeology in Bible Lands* (Chicago: Moody Press, 1977), p. 115; William White, Jr., "Babylon, City of," in *The New International Dictionary of Biblical Archaeology* (Grand Rapids, Mich.: Regency Reference Library, Zondervan Publishing House, 1983), p. 86.

3. Archer, "Daniel," p. 70.

these vessels and praising the false deities of Babylon (vv. 3–4). Soon, however, the festive atmosphere of the banquet came to a sudden end. "The fingers of a man's hand emerged [from nowhere] and began writing opposite the lampstand on the plaster of the wall of the king's palace, and the king saw the back of the hand that did the writing" (v. 5). As drunken Belshazzar stared at the words the hand had written, his "face grew pale, and his thoughts alarmed him; and his hip joints went slack, and his knees began knocking together" (v. 6). This terrifying scene must have caused the musicians to lay aside their instruments, the dancing girls to stand motionless, the waiters to stop in their tracks, and the banquet guests to become fearful as they sat still in their seats. Finally, Belshazzar "called aloud to bring in the conjurers, the Chaldeans and the diviners" so that they could read and interpret the mysterious inscription (v. 7a). But they could neither read it nor give its meaning, in spite of the great rewards the king promised for anyone who could decode it (vv. 7b–8). Their failure to do so prompted Belshazzar to become even more alarmed than he was before (v. 9). After learning of this incident, the queen—who was probably Belshazzar's mother and a daughter of Nebuchadnezzar—entered the banquet hall and told the king that Daniel would be able to interpret the writing on the wall (vv. 10–12). Apparently, eighty-year-old Daniel was in semiretirement at this time, possibly because of poor health (cf. 8:27). This would explain why Daniel was not at the feast as well as why he was not known by Belshazzar (5:13). Obviously, however, not everyone had forgotten about Daniel. The queen mother spoke of him as a man with " 'an extraordinary spirit, knowledge and insight' " and as possessing the divinely empowered ability to interpret dreams, explain enigmas, and solve difficult problems (v. 12). It appears that Daniel's godly lifestyle had remained untainted by the heathenish culture of Babylon. As a result, he still stood out as an individual who could be counted on to come through when no one else was able to.

III. A Man to Admire

When Daniel was brought before Belshazzar, the king told him that if he could read and interpret the inscription, he would be clothed in royal garments, receive a gold necklace, and be given " 'authority as the third ruler in the kingdom' " (v. 16). In other words, Belshazzar offered Daniel one of the highest positions of authority in Babylonia, second only to the co-regency of Belshazzar and Nabonidus. But Daniel would not be bought. He told the monarch, " 'Keep your gifts for yourself, or give your rewards to someone else; however, I will read the inscription to the king and make the interpretation known to him' " (v. 17). Daniel refused to be a man-pleaser; instead, he chose to continue being a faithful servant of God (cf. Gal. 1:10).

A. A review. Before Daniel revealed the message that was on the palace wall, he reviewed some history with Belshazzar. Daniel reminded the king of the greatness and power of Nebuchadnezzar's rule (Dan. 5:18–19). The prophet also recalled that when Belshazzar's grandfather had become proud and arrogant, " 'he was deposed from his royal throne, and his glory was taken away from him' " (v. 20). Then for seven years Nebuchadnezzar became like a crazed beast, living with wild donkeys and eating grass like cattle, " 'until he recognized that the Most High God is ruler over the realm of mankind, and that He sets over it whomever He wishes' " (v. 21). After recounting these events, Daniel spoke some biting words to Belshazzar:

> "Yet you, his son, Belshazzar, have not humbled your heart, even though you knew all this, but you have exalted yourself against the Lord of heaven; and they have brought the vessels of His house before you, and you and your nobles, your wives and your concubines have been drinking wine from them; and you have praised the gods of silver and gold, of bronze, iron, wood and stone, which do not see, hear or understand. But the God in whose hand are your life-breath and your ways, you have not glorified. Then the hand was sent from Him, and this inscription was written out." (vv. 22–24)

There it was. Daniel had finally said it. The mysterious writing was God's word of judgment on this prideful king. Perhaps Belshazzar had feared as much when he first saw the inscription. If so, his fears were now confirmed.

B. The revelation. Daniel wasted no time revealing the interpretation of the writing:

> "Now this is the inscription that was written out: 'MENĒ, MENĒ, TEKĒL, UPHARSIN.' This is the interpretation of the message: 'MENĒ'—God has numbered your kingdom and put an end to it. 'TEKĒL'—you have been weighed on the scales and found deficient. 'PERES'—your kingdom has been divided and given over to the Medes and Persians." (vv. 25–28; cf. Jer. 27:4–7)

IV. A Promotion to Ignore

After Daniel had delivered the message of divine judgment, Belshazzar promoted him as he had promised (Dan. 5:29). But the reward was an empty one. "That same night Belshazzar the Chaldean king was slain. So Darius the Mede received the kingdom at about the age of sixty-two" (vv. 30–31). Under the leadership of Cyrus's resourceful commander, Ugbaru, the Medo-Persian military conquered Babylon on the night of October 12, 539 B.C. Some eighty years later, Greek historian Herodotus recounted what happened:

> Hereupon the Persians who had been left for the purpose at Babylon by the river-side, entered the stream, which had now sunk [because the Persians had diverted it to a nearby lake] so as to reach midway up a man's thigh, and thus got into the town. Had the Babylonians been apprised of what Cyrus was about, or had they noticed their danger, they would never have allowed the Persians to enter the city, but would have destroyed them utterly; for they would have made fast all the street-gates which gave upon the river, and mounting upon the walls along both sides of the stream, would so have caught the enemy as it were in a trap. But, as it was, the Persians came upon them by surprise and took the city. Owing to the vast size of the place, the inhabitants of the central parts (as the residents at Babylon declare), long after the outer portions of the town were taken, knew nothing of what had [happened], but as they were engaged in a festival, continued dancing and revelling until they learnt the capture but [learnt of it] too certainly.[4]

V. A Message to Apply

We would be wise to consider two important truths that emerge from this story.

A. God's judgment may seem slow, but it is thorough.

Belshazzar's wicked rule was allowed to continue for several years before God brought it to an end. Out of His grace, He gave Belshazzar every opportunity to turn from his gods and commit his life to the Lord. But when Belshazzar tried to set himself up higher than God, he was deposed and killed. This incident tells us that although the Lord is patient, He will not withhold judgment forever (cf. 2 Pet. 3:3–10). Therefore, we dare not take His compassion for granted by living our lives as we choose rather than as He desires.

B. We should never underestimate the power of one godly life.

Daniel's highly respected reputation as a man of God persisted in a climate of idolatry, immorality, and treason. Because of this believer's faithfulness, the Lord was able to use him mightily to influence and confront a pagan empire. God wants to use His people similarly today, but they must be committed to serving Him regardless of the pressures to do

---

4. As quoted by Archer, "Daniel," p. 75.

otherwise. Are you willing to be His spokesperson? Then submit yourself completely to Him and seek to obey Him unreservedly.

Living Insights

Study One ■■■

"The handwriting on the wall"... a phrase so familiar it has become a modern-day cliché. But the event it describes in the Book of Daniel was no everyday incident to King Belshazzar. It made this monarch's face grow pale, his hip joints weaken, and his knees knock.

- Let's take a fresh look at Daniel 5. You have read the story of Belshazzar's demise in one translation of the Bible. Now let's look at the same account in some different versions of the Scriptures. If possible, locate some other translations—for example, the King James, the New International, or the New King James versions. As you reread the story in another rendition, certain things may come to your attention that you have never noticed. Before you begin reading, ask God to show you something new in this chapter that will be especially meaningful to you during this time in your life.

Living Insights

Study Two ■■■

The final application in this lesson is a potent one: *We should never underestimate the power of one godly life.* Most of us can think of someone who really inspired us to walk closer with the Lord.

- Who in your life stands out as an example of godliness? Does that individual know how they've influenced you? Take time to honor this person by doing something special for him or her. Whether by writing a note, giving a small gift, or making something especially for this person, let him or her know how they have affected your walk with God. Your expression of appreciation will likely be a welcome source of encouragement.

The Marks of Integrity
Daniel 6:1–16a

The story of Daniel in the lions' den is probably familiar to most of us. However, many of us may not recall *why* Daniel was sentenced to be killed by lions. We will learn in this lesson that he faced the penalty of death, not because he had done something wrong, but because he had done what was right in God's sight. Unfortunately, things are no different for us than they were for Daniel in this regard. In some cases, people are still rewarded for sinning, while others are punished for acting righteously. Our world is not characterized by fairness ... and it will not be, until the Lord Jesus Christ returns to earth and establishes His perfect Kingdom. Until then, we need to know how we can best represent Him in an unjust environment. Daniel 6:1–16a provides us with an excellent example of someone who was able to do this.

I. Some Introductory Matters

The historical setting for the events recorded in Daniel 6 is found in verses 30–31 of chapter 5. There we read about the death of King Belshazzar on the night Babylon fell to the Medo-Persian military forces. This event led to Darius the Mede receiving the Babylonian kingdom "at about the age of sixty-two" (5:31). Bible critics have argued that the author of Daniel confused Darius the Mede with Darius I, a Persian king who ruled a generation later (521–486 B.C.). But Old Testament scholar John C. Whitcomb has convincingly demonstrated from ancient documents that Darius the Mede was a subordinate under the Persian monarch Cyrus the Great. This viceroy's name was Gubaru, and his title was Darius the Mede—a unique honorific title that indicated his governorship over Babylonia. This identification fits well with the biblical text. For example, Daniel 5:31 says that "Darius the Mede *received* the kingdom" (emphasis added), indicating that he was given the authority to rule by someone greater than himself (cf. 9:1). Also, the Book of Daniel never refers to Darius the Mede as the king of Persia, but it does ascribe this title to Cyrus, which substantiates the fact that Darius was a viceroy of the king, not the king himself (cf. 9:1 and 11:1 with 10:1).[1] Keeping this background in mind, we are ready

---

1. One of the best discussions available on the identity of Darius the Mede is provided by John C. Whitcomb, Jr., in his book *Darius the Mede: The Historical Chronology of Daniel* (Nutley, N.J.: Presbyterian and Reformed Publishing Co., 1977). Some excellent, brief treatments of this issue can be found in these sources: Gleason L. Archer, *Encyclopedia of Bible Difficulties,* foreword by Kenneth S. Kantzer (Grand Rapids, Mich.: Zondervan Publishing House, 1982), pp. 286–88; Gleason L. Archer, Jr., "Daniel," in *The Expositor's Bible Commentary,* 12 vols., edited by Frank E. Gaebelein (Grand Rapids, Mich.: Regency Reference Library, Zondervan Publishing House, 1976–   ), vol. 7, pp. 16–19, 76–77.

to examine what the scriptural record tells us about the political situation during Gubaru's brief reign as governor of Babylonia and the prophet Daniel's involvement in it.

A. **The political situation.** In Daniel 6:1, we learn that Darius appointed "120 satraps over the [Babylonian] kingdom." John Whitcomb explains that "a 'satrap' was a Persian official who could rule over a large province or over a small group of people."[2] Darius also appointed three commissioners to oversee the satraps so "that the king might not suffer loss" (v. 2). Apparently, he was concerned that the delegation of authority to so many individuals could lead to the abuse of political power and the theft of state revenue.

B. **Daniel's role.** The text informs us that Darius chose eighty-year-old Daniel to be one of the three commissioners (v. 2a). "In view of Daniel's successful prediction in Belshazzar's banquet hall, it was only natural for Darius to select him for so responsible a position, though he was neither a Mede nor a Persian. His long experience and wide acquaintance with Babylonian government made Daniel an exceptionally qualified candidate."[3] Once Daniel became a governing official under Darius, he "began distinguishing himself among the commissioners and satraps because he possessed an *extraordinary spirit*" (v. 3a, emphasis added). This verse brings out the first of four marks of integrity that characterized Daniel's life—namely, an *excellent attitude.* In the biblical record there is no hint that Daniel felt threatened by or jealous of the other two commissioners. Instead, it appears that he maintained a positive, winsome, and teachable approach toward his new responsibilities. As a result, Darius planned to promote Daniel to a position of authority in Babylonia second only to his and that of King Cyrus (v. 3b).

> ### Some Personal Application
> What kind of attitude do you display on the job? Are you easy and enjoyable to work with? Do you manifest a willingness to learn? Or is your attitude toward your employer and fellow employees scarred by personal grudges, feelings of resentment, and envious thoughts?

2. John C. Whitcomb, *Daniel,* Everyman's Bible Commentary (Chicago: Moody Press, 1985), p. 81. In this book, Whitcomb adds that the *Nabonidus Chronicle,* a sixth-century B.C. extra-biblical document of historical events, states that Gubaru " 'installed sub-governors in Babylon' " (p. 80). This fits well with the biblical statement concerning the appointment of 120 satraps by Darius—an additional confirmation that Darius the Mede and Gubaru were the same individual.

3. Archer, "Daniel," p. 78.

> The Lord wants us to have an excellent attitude on the
> job . . . indeed, in whatever we do throughout life.

II. The Plot against Daniel

We might expect that Daniel's virtuous attitude at work and his
upcoming promotion would have brought cheers of praise from the
other government officials. But such was not the case. As we will
see, they made every attempt to get rid of him . . . and they almost
succeeded in their efforts.

A. Attempted accusations. The first avenue the satraps and
commissioners pursued in their efforts at removing Daniel from
office was to try to find grounds for accusing him "in regard to
government affairs" (v. 4a). They did everything they could to
find fault with Daniel's performance on the job. However, "they
could find no ground of accusation or evidence of corruption"
(v. 4b). His job record was spotless. How did he keep it so clean?
By remaining *faithful in his work* (v. 4c). This is the second mark
of integrity that Daniel displayed.

Some Personal Application
Proverbs 20:6 says, "Many a man proclaims his own
loyalty, / But who can find a trustworthy man?" A truly
honest and diligent worker is a rare find. Even Christians
frequently do not exemplify faithfulness in their work. Are
you an industrious, devoted employee? Could your job
performance withstand intense scrutiny, as Daniel's did? If
not, commit yourself today to become a dependable,
responsible employee to the glory of God (cf. Eph. 6:5–8,
Col. 3:22–24, 1 Tim. 6:1–2, Titus 2:9–14).

Scripture implies that the satraps and commissioners went
beyond Daniel's public life and investigated his personal world.
But they discovered "no negligence or corruption . . . *in him"*
(Dan. 6:4c, emphasis added). This passage indicates that Daniel
was characterized by *personal purity*—a third mark of his
integrity.

Some Personal Application
Do you say that you believe one thing, then contradict it
with your actions? Do you give people the appearance of
holiness when inwardly you are hiding and even cherishing
sin? The Lord exhorts us to strive for purity in both our
public and private worlds (James 1:22–27; 1 Pet. 1:14–16;
1 John 3:2–10, 17–18).

B. Written injunction. Unable to find fault in Daniel's public or private life, the satraps and commissioners initiated a plan that would pit Daniel's religious convictions against the Medo-Persian government (Dan. 6:5–6a). These officials came before Darius and told him that all his major governmental subordinates had agreed to disallow the worship of anyone except him for thirty days. They added that any violators of this injunction would be executed by being thrown into the lions' den (vv. 6–7). Of course, the satraps and commissioners lied when they told Darius that all the officials under him had consented to the enactment of this proposal, since Daniel had not been consulted. These vengeful officials urged the king to sign their document into law, and Darius complied, thereby making the injunction irrevocable according to Medo-Persian policy (vv. 8–9). As we will see, once Daniel learned that it had become a law, he steadfastly refused to obey it.

C. Exposure and prosecution. "When Daniel knew that the document was signed, he entered his house (now in his roof chamber he had windows open toward Jerusalem); and he continued kneeling . . . three times a day, praying and giving thanks before his God, as he had been doing previously" (v. 10). Daniel's relationship with the Lord was not crisis-oriented. He manifested and maintained a *consistent walk with God*—the fourth mark of integrity revealed in this account. This verse shows us that Daniel had a place where he regularly met with God in prayer. We also learn from this passage that Daniel's openness about his religious practices was not new. His upstairs windows at home were always open toward Jerusalem during prayer times. The reason for this was that the Jerusalem temple, though destroyed by the Babylonians, was considered by the Hebrews to be the center of God's earthly attention (cf. 2 Chron. 6:18–40, 7:11–16).

> **Some Personal Application**
>
> Do you meet with God daily, or only during emergencies? Have you made prayer and your relationship to God the number one priority in your life? Are you seeking to know God better and serve Him more faithfully? Because Daniel chose to develop and maintain a consistent walk with the Lord, he did not panic when his faith and life were laid on the line. Rather, he turned to God as he always had and placed his burdens in the Lord's hands. You can experience the peace Daniel must have had if you will put God first in your life.

As we might have expected, the satraps and commissioners wasted no time in discovering and exposing Daniel's disobedience. After reminding the king of the injunction he had signed into law, they disclosed Daniel's violation of it (Dan. 6:12b–13). When Darius heard the charge, "he was deeply distressed and set his mind on delivering Daniel; and even until sunset he kept exerting himself to rescue him" (v. 14). But Darius's governing officials were relentless. They came to the Medo-Persian viceroy and said, " 'Recognize, O king, that it is a law of the Medes and Persians that no injunction or statute which the king establishes may be changed' " (v. 15).

D. The ultimate consequence. Both Darius and Daniel had been legally trapped. No doubt, Daniel knew that the law would have to be carried out, but that did not stop him from disobeying it when it clashed with his religious convictions. And Darius, as the appointed ruler over the former Babylonian Empire, was bound by Medo-Persian law to obey the injunction he had approved. Therefore, the end was inevitable. "The king gave orders, and Daniel was brought in and cast into the lions' den" (v. 16a).

III. Some Practical Lessons

In the next lesson, we will discover what happened to Daniel after he was thrown into the den of lions. But from the part of the story we have read so far, we can glean three more truths that can help us find peace when we are ill-treated.

A. We will seldom receive what we deserve from people. Whether it is criticism or honor, the world usually will not pay what is due us. So we should learn not to expect it.

B. We will always receive what is best from God. Although it may not be according to our timetable, God will always supply us with what we need. So we should not doubt Him.

C. Our ability to handle human injustice and divine goodness is directly related to the consistency of our walk with God. Only if we have stability in our relationship with the Lord will we be able to accept man's unfair criticisms and wait for God's blessings.

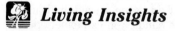 *Living Insights*

Study One

It's amazing how a person's integrity can surface in the midst of a crisis. Daniel's response to the new law is an excellent example of this very observation. The key issue is that Daniel went to the lions' den for doing right, not wrong!

- Peter's first epistle addresses the issue of suffering for doing what is right. Copy the following chart into your notebook and read the suggested passages. Then, write down the principles of integrity that you derive from these texts. If you make them part of your life, they will help you handle those situations in which you are persecuted for righteousness.

Marks of Integrity—1 Peter	
References	Principles
1:6–9	
2:11–12	
2:18–25	
3:13–22	
4:12–19	
5:6–10	

🌺 Living Insights

Study Two ▬▬▬▬▬▬▬▬▬▬▬▬▬▬▬▬▬▬▬▬▬▬▬▬▬

"Now when Daniel knew that the document was signed, he entered his house (now in his roof chamber he had windows open toward Jerusalem); and he continued kneeling ... three times a day, praying and giving thanks before his God, as he had been doing previously" (Dan. 6:10). Daniel showed integrity by consistently walking with God. How's your walk with Him?

- One way to measure the quality of our walk with God is by evaluating our daily devotional life. Take a few minutes to answer the following questions. Be honest with yourself.
  —What is involved in my daily devotions?
  —How consistent am I in doing them?
  —What priority do I give them?
  —Do I benefit from my time in the Word?
  —How effective is my prayer time?
  —How can I seek to improve my private meetings with God?

The Lions in Daniel's Den
Daniel 6:16b–28

The prophet Daniel's actions recorded in Daniel 6 perfectly illustrate the central instruction embedded in 1 Peter 2:13–20. For example, we are told in this New Testament letter to "submit [ourselves] for the Lord's sake to every human institution, whether to a king as the one in authority, or to governors as sent by him" (1 Pet. 2:13–14a). Daniel not only followed this principle, he surpassed it by distinguishing himself as a government official with an excellent attitude (Dan. 6:2–3). Again, in 1 Peter we read that our submission to political authority "is the will of God [and] that by doing right [we] may silence the ignorance of foolish men" (2:15). Daniel's political loyalty, fine job performance, and personal purity made it virtually impossible for his enemies to have him demoted or removed from office (Dan. 6:4). The First Epistle of Peter also tells us that God is pleased when "for the sake of conscience toward [Him] a man bears up under sorrows when suffering unjustly" (2:19). Daniel must have been troubled when he learned about the new law which disallowed the worship of anyone other than Darius for one month. But he refused to panic or slump into despair. Instead, Daniel went home and poured out his heart to God (Dan.6:10), well aware that this act of devotion to the Lord could bring swift and unmerciful punishment from the state. First Peter 2:20 adds: "For what credit is there if, when you sin and are harshly treated, you endure it with patience? But if when you do what is right and suffer for it you patiently endure it, this finds favor with God." Daniel was forced to face the lions' den for acting righteously before God. And, as we will see, he did so without complaint and with a clear conscience before Darius and the Lord. Daniel's response to this test of faith provides us with an example of how God wants us to handle our times of unjust suffering.

I. Daniel's Disobedience to Darius

The story of Daniel and the lions' den is as much about Darius as it is about Daniel. In fact, the ruler's response to Daniel's plight tells us a great deal about the friendship these men had. We also discover in this account that Darius had high regard for Daniel and his religious convictions. So as we focus on Daniel and his confrontation with death, let's pay particular attention to Darius and his response to Daniel's disobedience, punishment, and vindication.

A. Darius and Daniel. In the last lesson we learned that Darius tried everything possible to spare Daniel from execution (Dan. 6:14). But the law he had agreed to instate was clear: For thirty days, anyone who made a petition to any god or man other than Darius would be punished by death in the lions' den (v. 7b). Darius also realized that because he had established this law as King Cyrus's viceroy, it was irrevocable, according to

Medo-Persian policy. Therefore, he had no other legal alternative but to carry it out. So, soon after sunset, Darius commanded that Daniel be "cast into the lions' den" (v. 16a). Old Testament scholar C. F. Keil describes what archaeologists have discovered about lions' dens in ancient Morocco, giving us a good idea of their design during Darius's reign:

> [The Moroccan lions' dens] consist of a large square cavern under the earth, having a partition-wall in the middle of it, which is furnished with a door, which the keeper can open and close from above. By throwing in food they can entice the lions from the one chamber into the other, and then, having shut the door, they enter the vacant space for the purpose of cleaning it. The cavern is open above, its mouth being surrounded by a wall of a yard and a half high, over which one can look down into the den. This description agrees perfectly with that which is here given in the text [Dan. 6:16–17] regarding the lions' den.[1]

After Daniel was cast into the pit, Darius called down to him: " 'Your God whom you constantly serve will Himself deliver you' " (v. 16b). Although the Median ruler hoped for Daniel's deliverance, his trust in the God of Israel was not as great as his words to Daniel indicated (cf. vv. 18–20). The final step in the execution involved laying a heavy stone over the opening of the den and sealing it with moist clay tablets on which Darius and his nobles pressed their signet rings.[2] This official act meant that no one had the right to alter Daniel's execution in any way (v. 17). Once the punishment was carried out, "the king went off to his palace and spent the night fasting, and no entertainment was brought before him; and his sleep fled from him" (v. 18). Darius waited. All night he waited in anguish for the break of day. When the first rays of sunlight pierced the gray morning, he "went in haste to the lions' den" (v. 19). Removing the stone that covered the mouth of the den, Darius cried out with a troubled voice: " 'Daniel, servant of the living God, has your God, whom you constantly serve, been able to deliver you from the lions?' " (v. 20). Then, to the viceroy's relief and astonishment, came greetings from Daniel: " 'O king, live forever!' " (v. 21). The next words Daniel spoke conveyed a testimony of divine

1. C. F. Keil, *Biblical Commentary on the Book of Daniel,* translated by M. G. Easton (Grand Rapids, Mich.: William B. Eerdmans Publishing Co., n.d.), p. 216.

2. Gleason L. Archer, Jr., "Daniel," in *The Expositor's Bible Commentary,* 12 vols., edited by Frank E. Gaebelein (Grand Rapids, Mich.: Regency Reference Library, Zondervan Publishing House, 1976–   ), p. 81.

deliverance and vindication: " 'My God sent His angel and shut the lions' mouths, and they have not harmed me, inasmuch as I was found innocent before Him; and also toward you, O king, I have committed no crime' " (v. 22). We can discern from Daniel's comments that he was not anxious or fearful about being in the lions' den. Though still standing in the pit among the ferocious beasts, Daniel carried on a calm conversation with Darius, who was looking down on him from a position of safety. Overjoyed that he was alive, Darius "gave orders for Daniel to be taken up out of the den" (v. 23a). After he was helped out, Daniel was inspected for wounds, "but no injury whatever was found on him, because he had trusted in his God" (v. 23b). The Lord honored Daniel's loyalty to and faith in Him.

B. Darius and Daniel's enemies. Although Daniel did not retaliate against those who had plotted to have him killed, Darius did. The text describes the action he took: "The king ... gave orders, and they brought those men who had maliciously accused Daniel, and they cast them, their children, and their wives into the lions' den; and they had not reached the bottom of the den before the lions overpowered them and crushed all their bones" (v. 24). It is unlikely that this punishment included all the commissioners and satraps who served Darius. Probably, the only ones who suffered this awful fate were the ringleaders of the scheme to entrap Daniel.[3] As to the moral justification of including the conspirators' families in the punishment, John C. Whitcomb gives some biblical and historical insight:

> The God of Israel gave a law to His people through Moses that children should not "be put to death for their fathers; everyone shall be put to death for his own sin" (Deut. 24:16; cf. 2 Kings 14:6). If Achan's entire family was stoned to death for his sin, it was because all of them were active participants with the head of the household in this particular sin (Josh. 7:24–26).

> But the Medo-Persians had no such merciful law. Wives, children, and other relatives were often killed at the king's command when a man committed a serious crime against the royal house, thus "nipping in the bud" any possible retaliation by the criminal's family (to say nothing of the deterrent that such drastic justice would provide for potential enemies).[4]

3. See John F. Walvoord, *Daniel: The Key to Prophetic Revelation* (Chicago: Moody Press, 1971), p. 143.

4. John C. Whitcomb, *Daniel,* Everyman's Bible Commentary (Chicago: Moody Press, 1985), p. 88.

C. Darius and Daniel's God. Following the execution of Daniel's accusers, Darius composed and issued a decree "to all the peoples, nations, and men of every language who were living in all the land" (Dan. 6:25a). Consider what he said:

"May your peace abound! I make a decree that in all the dominion of my kingdom men are to fear and tremble before the God of Daniel;

For He is the living God and enduring forever,
And His kingdom is one which will not be destroyed,
And His dominion will be forever.
He delivers and rescues and performs signs and wonders
In heaven and on earth,
Who has also delivered Daniel from the power of the lions." (vv. 25b–27)

From that time forward, "Daniel enjoyed success in the reign of Darius and in the reign of Cyrus the Persian" (v. 28).

II. Our Response to Daniel's Test of Faith

This incredible story about Daniel's trust in God and his deliverance from death provides some counsel we need to remember when suffering mistreatment.

A. When persecuted falsely, trust God for deliverance. He may not always provide release when you want it and in the way you expect it, but He will always free you at the best time and in the best way.

B. When treated unjustly, wait for God to vindicate. He may not demonstrate your innocence as dramatically as He did Daniel's, but the Lord will make righteousness prevail according to His perfect plan.

C. When dealt with unfairly, allow God to retaliate. As the Apostle Paul says, "Never take your own revenge, beloved, but leave room for the wrath of God, for it is written, 'Vengeance is Mine, I will repay,' says the Lord" (Rom. 12:19).

D. When suffering undeservedly, let God use you to make Himself known to others. Daniel's faith testified to Darius, the Medo-Persian politicians, and the people of Babylonia that God is the eternal, all-powerful, sovereign Ruler over all. The Lord can also use *your* trust in Him to glorify Himself and bring others to a living, vital relationship with Him.

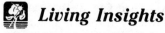
Living Insights

Study One ▬▬▬▬▬▬▬▬▬▬▬▬▬▬▬▬▬▬▬▬▬▬▬▬▬▬▬▬▬▬▬▬

There's no question about it, Daniel 6:16–28 tells one exciting story! It's a passage full of action words that detail the extraordinary account of a man facing a den full of lions.

- After copying this chart into your notebook, reread Daniel 6:16–28. In the left-hand column, write all the action words you discover in your reading. Then, in the right-hand column, write how each of these verbs help the text come alive to you.

Action Words—Daniel 6:16–28		
Verses	Action Words	Significance

Living Insights

Study Two ▬▬▬▬▬▬▬▬▬▬▬▬▬▬▬▬▬▬▬▬▬▬▬▬▬▬▬▬▬▬▬▬

What have been the "lions' den" experiences in your life? Most of us have been "thrown to the beasts" several times. But God delivered us, didn't He.

- Let's use this Living Insights to offer praise and gratitude to God for His faithful deliverance through the years. Give the Lord thanks for the marvelous works He has done in your life. If you are in a "lions' den" at this very moment, ask God for the strength to endure until He chooses to provide a way of escape. Remember even now to praise Him for His sovereign control over your life.

My Lions' Den Experiences

Past Trials	God's Deliverances

Present Struggle	My Prayer for God's Help

A Prophetic Collage
Daniel 7

In the first six chapters of the Book of Daniel, we become acquainted with the prophet Daniel, who emerged as God's spokesman in the Babylonian and Medo-Persian empires. The last six chapters of the book, however, focus not on Daniel's life but on the prophetic revelations he received from God. In this section of Scripture, we will find strange visions that unveil God's future program to man. These unusual prophecies were never intended to answer all our questions about what is to come. However, they do give us a panoramic perspective of what God has in store for both believers and unbelievers. The vision detailed in Daniel 7 is the first of these prophecies. It falls neatly into three parts that together convey one central message. Although this prophecy appears to be a confusing collection of animals, persons, nations, and events, it is actually a harmonious collage of the Lord's sovereign activity in human history.

I. An Overview of Daniel 7
Before we delve into the particulars of Daniel 7, let's take a look at its chronological placement in history, its literary structure, and its relationship to chapter 2 of Daniel.

A. Chronologically. We know from the first verse of Daniel 7 that the vision recorded in this chapter came to Daniel during "the first year of Belshazzar king of Babylon." This tells us that the vision was received around 553 B.C., when Daniel was about sixty-seven years old and still living under Babylonian rule.

B. Structurally. The vision in Daniel 7 can be divided into three sections that each begin with the words *I was looking* or *I kept looking.* The first section is comprised of verses 2–8. This passage talks about wind, water, and odd-looking beasts. Verses 9–12 form the next division, and they tell about thrones and judgment. The last segment, verses 13–27, relates the interpretation of the vision.

C. Comparatively. As we come to understand the vision and its meaning, we will discover that it parallels King Nebuchadnezzar's dream, which is revealed and interpreted in Daniel 2. We will note the similarities between the two as we analyze the details of Daniel 7.

II. The Vision Revealed
The text informs us that "Daniel saw a dream and visions in his mind as he lay on his bed; then he wrote the dream down and related the following summary of it" (Dan. 7:1). Let's examine what Daniel saw.

A. Part one: Winds and animals. We are first told that Daniel witnessed " 'the four winds of heaven . . . stirring up the great sea' " (v. 2b). The Hebrew word translated *winds* may also be rendered *spirits,* and thereby refer to angels. This term is often used in Scripture in connection with God's sovereign actions in human history as carried out by angelic beings (cf. Jer. 49:36, 51:1; Zech. 6:1–6, 7:14). The *great sea* may refer to either the Mediterranean Sea (cf. Num. 34:6–7, Josh. 1:4, Ezek. 48:28) or the peoples and nations of the world (cf. Rev. 17:15). If the latter is in view, and it most likely is, then Daniel is picturing humanity in the throes of a great upheaval that is being caused by angels of judgment (cf. Rev. 7:1–3, 9:13–19). Next, Daniel sees four strange beasts emerge from the sea (Dan. 7:3):

> "The first was like a lion and had the wings of an eagle. I kept looking until its wings were plucked, and it was lifted up from the ground and made to stand on two feet like a man; a human mind also was given to it. And behold, another beast, a second one, resembling a bear. And it was raised up on one side, and three ribs were in its mouth between its teeth; and thus they said to it, 'Arise, devour much meat!' After this I kept looking, and behold, another one, like a leopard, which had on its back four wings of a bird; the beast also had four heads, and dominion was given to it. After this I kept looking in the night visions, and behold, a fourth beast, dreadful and terrifying and extremely strong; and it had large iron teeth. It devoured and crushed, and trampled down the remainder with its feet; and it was different from all the beasts that were before it, and it had ten horns."
> (vv. 4–7)

While Daniel was meditating on the ten horns of the fourth beast, he saw another horn—initially smaller than the others—grow among the ten horns and eventually uproot three of them (v. 8a). " 'This horn,' " Daniel said, " 'possessed eyes like the eyes of a man, and a mouth uttering great boasts' " (v. 8b).

B. Part two: Thrones and judgment. As Daniel kept watching, he saw thrones being established and " 'the Ancient of Days [taking] His seat' " (v. 9a). This divine Person wore a snow-white vesture and had hair like pure wool (v. 9b). Furthermore,

> "His throne was ablaze with flames,
> Its wheels were a burning fire.
> A river of fire was flowing
> And coming out from before Him;
> Thousands upon thousands were attending Him,

And myriads upon myriads were standing before
Him." (vv. 9c–10a)

While this mighty Judge sat on His throne, " 'the books were
opened' " in His court (v. 10b). "Then," Daniel adds,

> "I kept looking because of the sound of the boastful
> words which the [eleventh] horn was speaking; I kept
> looking until the beast was slain, and its body was
> destroyed and given to the burning fire. As for the
> rest of the beasts, their dominion was taken away,
> but an extension of life was granted to them for an
> appointed period of time." (vv. 11–12)

As Daniel continued to watch the strange vision unfold, he saw
" 'One like a Son of Man' " brought into the presence of the
Ancient of Days (v. 13). The Ancient of Days glorified the Son of
Man and gave Him an indestructible and everlasting dominion
over all the earth so " 'that all the peoples, nations, and men of
every language / Might serve Him' " (v. 14).

C. **Part three: Intervention and interpretation.** What
Daniel had witnessed up to this point disturbed him deeply
(v. 15). In an attempt to get some clarification of the vision,
he asked someone next to him—perhaps the angel Gabriel
(cf. 8:16, 9:21)—to interpret the vision (7:16a). This individual
then explained to Daniel the events he had seen (v. 16b). Let's
examine the interpretation in detail.

1. **The four beasts.** The interpreter told Daniel that the great
beasts in his vision represented " ' "four kings who will arise
from the earth" ' " (v. 17). Although the interpreter does not
identify the four kings, it is clear that they refer to the four
kingdoms revealed in Nebuchadnezzar's dream of the statue
(Dan. 2). Therefore, the first beast—a lion with eagle's
wings—stands for the Babylonian Empire (7:4; cf. 2:37–38).
Throughout history, the lion has been a common symbol of
royal power. For example, King Solomon had twelve lion
monuments that lined the steps leading up to his throne
(1 Kings 10:20, 2 Chron. 9:19). And, interestingly, the gates
of the royal palaces of the Babylonians were guarded by
statues of winged lions. Moreover, the Scriptures often use
the lion and the eagle as symbols of Babylon (Jer. 4:7,
Ezek. 17:3). In Daniel's vision, the second beast—one that
resembles a bear, an animal of formidable strength—
represents the Medo-Persian Empire (Dan. 7:5; cf. 2:39a). We
know from both history and the Bible that the Medo-Persian
army was strong and fierce (Isa. 13:15–18). But unlike the
lion, which possesses a royal grace, the bear is ponderous
and ungainly in its movements. In this sense, the Medo-

Persian Empire was inferior to the kingdom of Babylonia. Daniel also saw that the bear was lopsided—apparently, an indication that the union between the Persians and the Medes was not an equal one. The Persians were greater and stronger than the Medes and eventually absorbed them into the Persian culture and political system. The third beast Daniel saw—namely, a winged leopard—symbolizes the Greek Empire (Dan. 7:6; cf. 2:39b). Concerning this identification, Bible scholar John F. Walvoord writes:

> The leopard in contrast to the lion, the first beast, is less grand and majestic, but it is swifter and was much feared as an animal of prey in Old Testament times. The swiftness of the leopard made it the standard of comparison in Habakkuk 1:8 where the horses of the Chaldeans are described as swifter than leopards. Leopards characteristically would lie in wait for their prey (Jer 5:6; Ho 13:7) and then pounce upon their victims with great speed and agility....
>
> The impression of great speed inherent in a leopard is further enhanced by the presence of four wings on its back....
>
> With the swiftness of a leopard, Alexander the Great conquered most of the civilized world all the way from Macedonia to Africa and eastward to India. The lightning character of his conquests is without precedent in the ancient world, and this is fully in keeping with the image of speed embodied in the leopard itself and the four wings on its back.[1]

After the death of Alexander the Great, four kings rose to power and subdivided the Grecian kingdom. "These four kings and their reigns were ... Lysimachus, who held Thrace and Bithynia; Cassander, who held Macedonia and Greece; Seleucus, who controlled Syria, Babylonia, and territories as far east as India; and Ptolemy, who controlled Egypt, Palestine, and Arabia Petrea."[2] The fourth beast in Daniel's vision represents the Roman Empire and the Western nations that grew out of it and continued to manifest its influence (Dan. 7:7; cf. 2:40–43). Perhaps to ease Daniel's fears, the interpreter told him that " ' "the saints of the

1. John F. Walvoord, *Daniel: The Key to Prophetic Revelation* (Chicago: Moody Press, 1971), p. 157.
2. Walvoord, *Daniel,* p. 158.

Highest One will receive the kingdom and possess the kingdom forever, for all ages to come" ' " (7:18). In other words, the dominion of the fourth kingdom will come to an end and be replaced by God's kingdom, which will last forever and be governed by His people.

2. The fourth beast. After being consoled that believers would one day rule with the Lord, Daniel inquired further about the dreadful fourth beast, the ten horns on its head, and the eleventh horn that grew up among the others and subdued three of them (vv. 19–20a). This eleventh horn, said Daniel, " 'had eyes and a mouth uttering great boasts, and ... was larger in appearance than its associates' " (v. 20b). Furthermore, this horn " 'was waging war with the saints and overpowering them until the Ancient of Days came, and judgment was passed in favor of the saints of the Highest One, and the time arrived when the saints took possession of the kingdom' " (vv. 21b–22). In response to Daniel's request, the interpreter explained what the fourth beast represents—a fourth earthly kingdom that differs from the other three and " ' "will devour the whole earth and tread it down and crush it" ' " (v. 23). To a limited degree, this occurred when the Romans methodically conquered and ruled over much of the then-known world. However, the mention of the whole earth in this passage indicates a worldwide kingdom that surpasses the boundaries of ancient Rome, yet possesses distinctive characteristics of Rome's power and prestige. From this incredible empire, " ' "ten kings will arise; and another will arise after them, and he will be different from the previous ones and will subdue three kings" ' " (v. 24). When the Roman Empire was conquered in the fifth century A.D., individual nations, not a united empire, arose from its ruins. These Western nations have remained divided to this day, but they will not stay independent forever. At some future time, ten nations will lock arms politically, economically, and militarily, forming a revived or realigned Roman Empire. However, a leader will emerge from their midst, gain power, and take control of three of these nations in his initial rise to world domination. He will oppose God's authority, oppress His saints, and "introduce an entirely new era in which he will abandon all previous laws and institute his own system"[3] (v. 25a). This world dictator is the Antichrist, who is described in the New

---

3. J. Dwight Pentecost, "Daniel," in *The Bible Knowledge Commentary: Old Testament Edition,* edited by John F. Walvoord and Roy B. Zuck (Wheaton, Ill.: Victor Books, 1985), p. 1354.

Testament as "the man of lawlessness" and as a satanically empowered beast (cf. 2 Thess. 2:3–10; Rev. 13, 17). He will have power over believers " ' "for a time, times, and half a time" ' " (Dan. 7:25b)—that is, for three and a half years. The New Testament reveals that this consists of the last half of the seven-year Tribulation (Rev. 11:1–3, 13:5–7; cf. Dan. 9:27). The oppressive rule of the Antichrist will end when Christ returns in power to establish His Millennial Kingdom on earth (Dan. 7:13–14, 26–27; cf. Rev. 19:11–20:2). After this event was explained to Daniel, " 'the revelation ended,' " leaving him pale and greatly alarmed (Dan. 7:28).

III. The Vision Applied

This incredible vision has much to teach us. Among the many lessons we can learn, four are especially relevant. Two of them are historically oriented, and the other two are more personal. Let's briefly consider each one.

A. Since the predictions concerning the first three kingdoms have come true, we can be sure that all the details related to the fourth one will come to pass. God will accomplish what He says He will do. Our records of the past bear this out.

B. Since the nations are established by God, they dwell under His sovereign control. The countries of the world cannot do anything to postpone or cancel the outworking of His plan. History has proved this time and time again.

C. The God who has mapped out our future is certainly able to handle the present. Though it may seem at times that the Lord has abandoned us, He has promised He will never forsake us (Heb. 13:5–6).

D. Although life may appear to be a confusing collage, it is in reality the perfect unfolding of an infallible, divine plan. So we can be comforted in the fact that God has matters under control as He seeks to prepare us for a life of glory in His Kingdom.

Living Insights

Study One

Serious students of Bible prophecy can see the connection between chapters 2 and 7 of Daniel. It would be well worth our time to compare these two great texts even more closely.

* Review Daniel 2:31–45, 7:1–27, and the study guide lessons that correspond to these references. Write down everything you can find

out about the ruling powers these chapters describe. A copy of this chart will serve as a handy tool for categorizing your discoveries.

Ruling Powers—Daniel 2 and 7	
Kingdoms	Descriptions
1. Babylonia	
2. Medo-Persia	
3. Greece	
4. Rome	
5. Millennium	

Living Insights

Study Two

A *collage* is "an artistic composition made of various materials glued on a picture surface."[4] We have examined a prophetic collage; now let's look at a personal one.

- What would a collage of your life look like? Brainstorm on this idea for a while, focusing on what God has brought you through and how He has changed you. You may want to put together an actual collage with photos, magazine pictures, newspaper headlines, diary entries, and the like. A project of this nature can visually reveal God's hand in your life and, as a result, greatly encourage your growth in Him.

4. *Webster's Ninth New Collegiate Dictionary*, s.v. "collage."

The Final World Dictator
Selected Scripture

In Daniel 7, we surveyed some key events in God's plan for the future. Included in this overview was a strange yet important detail—the growth and dominating influence of a small horn among ten other horns. We discovered that this eleventh horn represents a person with dynamic leadership ability and power who will become the last world dictator. Because this individual will play such a strategic role in the events still to come, we would be wise to supplement our knowledge of him with relevant information from biblical passages other than Daniel 7. As we do, we will gain a more complete picture of the terrible events that will precede Christ's millennial reign of peace and prosperity.

I. A Comforting Fact about the Rapture

Before the Great Tribulation occurs and the Antichrist rises to world prominence, *God will remove all believers from the earth.* Several biblical passages bear out this truth, but two are especially significant. In Revelation 3:10, we read Christ's words to the Philadelphian believers: " 'Because you have kept the word of My perseverance, I also will keep you from the hour of testing, that hour which is about to come upon the whole world, to test those who dwell upon the earth.' " The Greek expression translated *keep from* means "to preserve something outside the sphere of something else." Therefore, Jesus is telling the Christians of the Philadelphian church that He will protect them from the worldwide testing by keeping them away from it.[1] The "hour of testing" Christ is referring to is the Tribulation—a seven-year time span of severe, divine judgment that will affect the entire earth. This catastrophic period is described in Revelation 6–19. In Paul's first letter to the Thessalonian believers, he explains how the Lord will remove His people before the rest of the world experiences this awesome outpouring of God's wrath:

> If we believe that Jesus died and rose again, even so God will bring with Him those who have fallen asleep in Jesus. For this we say to you by the word of the Lord, that we who are alive, and remain until the coming of the Lord, shall not precede those who have fallen asleep [i.e., died]. For the Lord Himself will descend from heaven with a shout, with the voice of the archangel, and with the trumpet of God; and the dead in Christ shall rise first. Then we who are alive and remain shall be caught

---

1. Jeffrey L. Townsend substantiates this understanding in his article "The Rapture in Revelation 3:10," *Bibliotheca Sacra* 137:547 (July–September 1980), pp. 252–66.

up together with them in the clouds to meet the Lord in the air, and thus we shall always be with the Lord. (1 Thess. 4:14–17)

This event is commonly referred to as the Rapture. Once it occurs, only unbelievers will be left on the earth to experience divine judgment, and believers will revel with joy as they commune with Christ in heaven.[2] Although non-Christians find no pleasure in this prediction, Christians can "comfort one another with these [prophetic] words" (v. 18).

II. Some General Information about the Antichrist

If we were to skim books and listen to talks on biblical prophecy, we would find several misconceptions about the Antichrist that would need to be dispelled. So let's briefly consider some facts about this man that are thoroughly grounded in God's inerrant Word.

A. He will be wanted, not rejected. Throughout time, people have followed even devious men and women who made promises to give them what they wanted. This kind of blind, selfish devotion has frequently developed in countries that have experienced political, economic, moral, and religious deterioration. In such turmoil, false messiahs and tyrannical rulers have historically gained popular approval that they may not have otherwise had. It is likely that the Antichrist's rise to power will come during a time when people are longing for deliverance from tumultuous days.

B. He will be appealing, not repulsive. Although the Antichrist will have a spiteful, beast-like nature, he will not be beastly in appearance. Nor will he be offensive in conduct—at least not initially. Instead, he will have an uncanny charisma that will win people over to his side.

C. He will be extraordinary, not ordinary. He will have the oratorical skill of a John Kennedy, the inspirational power of a Winston Churchill, the determination of a Joseph Stalin, the vision of a Karl Marx, the respectability of a Ghandi, the military prowess of a Douglas MacArthur, the charm of a Will Rogers, and the genius of a King Solomon. In addition, he will be empowered by Satan, and his incredible capabilities will be used against God's people.

---

2. Three positions have generally been taken concerning the relationship between the Rapture and the Tribulation: pretribulationism, midtribulationism, and posttribulationism. Insight for Living has adopted a pretribulational position. If you would like to explore these viewpoints in greater depth, we would recommend that you consult the study guide titled *Contagious Christianity: A Study of First Thessalonians*, edited by Bill Watkins, from the Bible-teaching ministry of Charles R. Swindoll (Fullerton, Calif.: Insight for Living, 1985), pp. 44–56.

D. He will be a Gentile, not a Jew. Daniel 7 indicates that the Antichrist will come from the divided Roman Empire, which is Gentile in origin (vv. 2–3, 7–8, 19–25).

III. Several Specific Scriptures Describing the Antichrist

Perusing the pages of Scripture, we find four passages that contribute a great deal to our understanding of the Antichrist.

A. Daniel 7. This chapter tells us that the final world dictator will rise to power out of the natural flow of events (v. 24). That is, the stage will be set for him to put his insidious scheme for world domination into motion. This opportunity will occur shortly after the Rapture. Furthermore, his religious position will not be a secret. " ' "He will speak out against the Most High" ' " and persecute those who become Christians during the Tribulation (v. 25a). As a political despot, he will even abolish all previous laws and institute his own anti-God standards (v. 25b).

B. Second Thessalonians 2. In this letter Paul attempts to settle the worries of the Thessalonian believers concerning the Second Advent of Christ. These Christians had heard that the Lord had already returned to rule over the nations (vv. 1–2). So Paul informs them that this event will *not* occur until "the apostasy comes . . . , and the man of lawlessness is revealed, the son of destruction" (v. 3). In this context, the term *apostasy* refers to a period in which the world will make a dramatic turn away from God's standards and spurn His revealed counsel (cf. 1 Tim. 4:1–3; 2 Tim. 3:1–5, 4:3–4; 2 Pet. 2, 3:3–6; Jude). During this time of heightened rebellion, the one who epitomizes sin and whose end is everlasting destruction will be unveiled. He will oppose Christianity and all other religions as well as "[exalt] himself above every so-called god or object of worship" (2 Thess. 2:4a). He will even sit on God's throne in the inner sanctuary of the temple in Jerusalem and claim to be the Lord Himself (v. 4b).

C. Revelation 13. This passage of Scripture identifies the Antichrist as the ruler of the revived Roman Empire (v. 1; cf. 17:7, 12–13; Dan. 7:7–8). Many of the characteristics of the Greek, Medo-Persian, and Babylonian empires will be evident in him and his rule (Rev. 13:2a; cf. Dan. 7:4–6). But he will not be humanly or divinely empowered. The text says that the source of his power, prestige, and authority will be "the dragon"—that is, Satan himself (Rev. 13:2b; cf. 20:2). At some point before the ultimate height of his career, the Antichrist will receive a wound that would normally be fatal. But instead of dying from the injury, he will be miraculously healed by Satan. This seemingly supernatural event will amaze the people of the world and prompt them to follow the Antichrist (13:3). The Bible adds that the people will worship Satan "because he gave his authority to the beast," and they will worship the Antichrist, "saying, 'Who is like the beast, and who is able to wage war with him?'" (v. 4; cf. v. 8). This wicked ruler will have an accomplice—a false prophet who will also operate with satanic authority and support the worship and rule of the Antichrist (vv. 11–12). The false prophet will perform counterfeit miracles that will deceive the masses into worshiping an image of the world dictator (vv. 13–15a). Anyone who refuses to bow down before this image will be killed (v. 15b). The Antichrist's conspirator will demand that everyone receive "a mark on their right hand, or on their forehead" (v. 16). This mark will be "either the name of the beast or the number of his name," which is "six hundred and sixty-six" (vv. 17b, 18b). Concerning the speculative calculation of this number, John F. Walvoord gives some helpful comments:

> There has been much speculation on the insignia or "mark" of the beast, but it could be any of several kinds of identification. Countless attempts have been made to interpret the number 666, usually using the numerical equivalents of letters in the Hebrew, Greek, or other alphabets. As there probably have been hundreds of explanations continuing down to the present day, it is obvious that if the number refers to an individual it is not clear to whom it refers.
>
> Probably the best interpretation is that the number six is one less than the perfect number seven, and the threefold repetition of the six would indicate that for all their pretentions to deity, Satan and the two beasts were just creatures and not the Creator.[3]

D. Revelation 19. The dethronement and demise of the Antichrist and the false prophet will occur at the Second Coming of Christ. When the world dictator, the nations' leaders, and their military forces are assembled at Armageddon to fight against Christ and His army, the Lord will capture the Antichrist and his false prophet and throw them "alive into the lake of fire which burns with brimstone" (vv. 19–20). Christ will also destroy the armies present at Armageddon and other non-Christians scattered elsewhere around the globe (vv. 17–18, 21; cf. Matt. 24:29–51).

---

3. John F. Walvoord, "Revelation," in *The Bible Knowledge Commentary: New Testament Edition*, edited by John F. Walvoord and Roy B. Zuck (Wheaton, Ill.: Victor Books, 1983), p. 963.

IV. A Few Concluding Suggestions regarding the Antichrist

Certainly, many of the events described in these passages are horrible, but if we are trusting in Jesus Christ as our Savior and Lord, we need not expect them with fear. After all, He will take all Christians to be with Him *prior* to the Tribulation and the Antichrist's ascension to power. However, the Lord does exhort us to stay alert in our spiritual walk as we watch for His imminent return to rapture the Church (Matt. 25:1–30). In obedience to this, there are at least three things we can do.

A. Watch the news with our eyes on the Middle East.

B. Interpret current events with our minds on prophetic truth.

C. Anticipate Christ's return with our hearts on God's promise—the Rapture of the Church.

 Living Insights

Study One

Just as the Book of Daniel is the hub of Old Testament prophecy, Revelation is the key work of prophecy in the New Testament. And, as this lesson points out, Revelation 13 describes the Antichrist in greater detail than Daniel 7 does. Given this, let's look at Revelation 13 more closely.

- Read through the eighteen verses of Revelation 13, paying special attention to the symbolic language used in describing the Antichrist. Then, on a copy of the chart below, jot down the images, or word pictures, you discover. What do they represent? Can you figure out their interpretations? Try to derive the meaning of each symbol from the context immediately surrounding it, where the interpretation is often clearly presented.

The Antichrist in Revelation 13		
Verses	Images	Interpretations

Continued on next page

🪷 *Living Insights*

The next event on God's great calendar is the removal of all believers from the earth. Are you ready for the Rapture of the Church? Do you know anyone who is not?

- It's difficult to study future events without becoming burdened for someone who doesn't know Christ. Who has God placed on your heart?

- Begin praying specifically for that person's salvation. Ask God to provide an opportunity for you to present Christ to this lost individual.

- Before you share the gospel with this person, demonstrate it to him or her by doing an unsolicited act of kindness—such as washing a car, mowing a lawn, baking a pie, or sending flowers—to show the love of Christ and prepare that friend to hear His message.

The Living End
Daniel 8

In our study of the Book of Daniel, we have seen that most of what was future to Daniel is now history to us. The prophecy in the eighth chapter of this book is a case in point. However, even though it speaks of events that have already transpired, we would be mistaken to label it irrelevant or boring. Indeed, it is amazing to realize that the events prophesied in Daniel 8 were revealed centuries before they actually took place. Moreover, interwoven with the fulfilled prophecy of this chapter is a prediction that has only been partially fulfilled so far. Its ultimate completion could occur in *our* century. Now that's relevant! So let's blow the dust off this ancient passage of Scripture and pay attention to its message. In doing so, we will discover some insight that will help us live better today as we look toward tomorrow.

I. The Vision

According to the scriptural account, Daniel received a second vision "in the third year of the reign of Belshazzar the king." This was approximately two years after Daniel saw the vision of the four beasts (7:1)—a fact that places the revelation of his second vision around 551 B.C., when he was close to seventy years old. We also discover that in his vision Daniel saw himself "in the citadel of Susa, which is in the province of Elam" (8:2a). The royal city of Susa was 350 miles east of Babylon—the capital city in which Daniel lived at this time—and it was the birthplace of the Medo-Persian Empire. Susa was also the headquarters of the Persian king Cyrus. Daniel says that he saw himself "beside the Ulai Canal" (v. 2b)—a man-made irrigation ditch that ran near Susa. As the vision continued to unfold, Daniel observed a two-horned ram "standing in front of the canal" (v. 3a). Both of the ram's horns were long, "but one was longer than the other, with the longer one coming up last" (v. 3b). Apparently, this ram came from the east and butted "westward, northward, and southward" (v. 4a). His assaults were so potent that "no other beasts could stand before him, nor was there anyone to rescue from his power" (v. 4b). Indeed, "he did as he pleased and magnified himself" (v. 4c). As Daniel kept looking, he saw "a male goat . . . coming from the west over the surface of the whole earth without touching the ground; and the goat had a conspicuous horn between his eyes" (v. 5). This goat rushed at the ram "in his mighty wrath" and "struck the ram and shattered his two horns" (vv. 6–7a). Unable to withstand the goat's attack or find deliverance from his incredible strength, the ram was hurled to the ground and trampled underfoot (v. 7). "Then the male goat magnified himself exceedingly. But as soon as he was mighty, the large horn was broken; and in its place there

75

came up four conspicuous horns toward the four winds of heaven"
(v. 8). A smaller horn came out of one of these horns and "grew
exceedingly great toward the south, toward the east, and toward the
Beautiful Land" (v. 9)—that is, toward Israel.

> And [this horn] grew up to the host of heaven and caused
> some of the host and some of the stars to fall to the earth,
> and it trampled them down. It even magnified itself to be
> equal with the Commander of the host; and it removed
> the regular sacrifice from Him, and the place of His
> sanctuary was thrown down. And on account of trans-
> gression the host will be given over to the horn along
> with the regular sacrifice; and it will fling truth to the
> ground and perform its will and prosper. Then I heard a
> holy one speaking, and another holy one said to that
> particular one who was speaking, "How long will the
> vision about the regular sacrifice apply, while the
> transgression causes horror, so as to allow both the holy
> place and the host to be trampled?" And he said to me,
> "For 2,300 evenings and mornings; then the holy place
> will be properly restored." (vv. 10–14)

The phrase "2,300 evenings and mornings" could indicate 2,300
twenty-four-hour days or 1,150 days, each composed of one evening
and one morning. However, this phrase occurs in a context that tells
about the suspension of temple sacrifices, which were traditionally
offered each morning and evening; therefore, the reference most
likely denotes 1,150 days.[1] In other words, Daniel was told that a
time would come when the little horn would make itself out to be
equal with God and, as a result, would halt all temple sacrifices for
three years and fifty-five days. At the end of this period, however,
the worship of God in the temple would resume.

II. The Interpretation

Once this vision was revealed to Daniel, he "sought to understand
it" (8:15a). Then he encountered one who was called on to interpret
it for him. This angelic messenger was Gabriel (v. 16), who was later
involved in the birth announcements of both John the Baptist and
Jesus of Nazareth (Luke 1:8–20, 26–38). When Gabriel came close
to Daniel, the prophet became fearful and fell with his face to the
ground (Dan. 8:17a). Gabriel issued no words of consolation; instead,
he informed Daniel that " 'the vision pertains to the time of the end' "
(v. 17b), " 'the final period of the indignation' " (v. 19b). As we will

---

1. Gleason L. Archer, Jr., "Daniel," in *The Expositor's Bible Commentary*, 12 vols., edited by
Frank E. Gaebelein (Grand Rapids, Mich.: Regency Reference Library, Zondervan Publishing
House, 1976–   ), vol. 7, p. 103.

see, some elements of the vision manifest the interpretive "law of double fulfillment." That is, the vision describes a person who lived and died several centuries after Daniel's lifetime and who foreshadows another individual yet to arrive on the scene. Let's now examine the details of Gabriel's interpretation.

A. **The identity of the ram.** Gabriel first explained that the two-horned ram " 'represents the kings of Media and Persia' " (v. 20). History bears out that "the guardian spirit of the Persian kingdom [appeared] under the form of a ram with clean feet and sharp-pointed horns, and . . . the Persian king, when he stood at the head of his army, bore . . . the head of a ram."[2] Historical records also confirm that the Persians grew in power and influence later than the Medes, and that they eventually dominated the Medes under the leadership of Cyrus in the sixth century B.C. Cyrus's greatest military movements, as well as those of his successors, expanded the Medo-Persian Empire north toward the Caspian Sea, west toward Asia Minor and Greece, and south toward Babylonia, Israel, and Egypt.

B. **The identity of the goat.** The angel Gabriel further noted that " 'the shaggy goat represents the kingdom of Greece, and the large horn that is between his eyes is the first king' " (v. 21). This Grecian monarch was Alexander the Great, who, with an army of only forty thousand men, conquered the Medo-Persian Empire even to the borders of India in an amazingly short period of time (334–326 B.C.). "Having carved out an empire of 1.5 million square miles, Alexander provoked many of his Macedonian leaders to rebellion by claiming to be a god, by merging Persian and Greek elements in his army, and by marrying Persian women."[3] In 323, Alexander entered Babylon for the last time. " 'Worn out by wounds, hardship and overdrinking, he fell ill of a fever. Soon he could neither move nor speak. He was propped up and each officer and soldier filed past. He acknowledged each man with his eyes or a slight movement of his head. Within two days Alexander died. He was not yet thirty-three years old.' "[4]

C. **The identity of the four horns.** Gabriel added that the four horns which arose in place of the broken horn—Alexander the Great—" 'represent four kingdoms which will arise from his

2. C. F. Keil, *Biblical Commentary on the Book of Daniel,* translated by M. G. Easton (Grand Rapids, Mich.: William B. Eerdmans Publishing Co., n.d.), p. 290.

3. John C. Whitcomb, *Daniel,* Everyman's Bible Commentary (Chicago: Moody Press, 1985), p. 110.

4. *Greece and Rome* (Washington, D.C.: National Geographic Society, 1968), p. 246 as quoted by Whitcomb, *Daniel,* p. 110.

nation, although not with his power'" (v. 22). After Alexander died, efforts were made to hold his kingdom together, but they all failed. Eventually, four of his generals divided the Grecian Empire four ways. Cassander governed Macedonia and Greece; Lysimachus controlled Thrace and the western half of Asia Minor; Ptolemy ruled over Egypt, northern Africa, Palestine, Cilicia, and Cyprus; and Seleucus exercised authority over the rest of Asia all the way to the Indus Valley.[5]

D. The past identity of the little horn. Gabriel then explained to Daniel about the small horn that came from one of the four horns:

> "And in the latter period of their rule,
> When the transgressors have run their course,
> A king will arise
> Insolent and skilled in intrigue.
> And his power will be mighty, but not by his own power,
> And he will destroy to an extraordinary degree
> And prosper and perform his will;
> He will destroy mighty men and the holy people.
> And through his shrewdness
> He will cause deceit to succeed by his influence;
> And he will magnify himself in his heart,
> And he will destroy many while they are at ease.
> He will even oppose the Prince of princes,
> But he will be broken without human agency."
> (vv. 23–25)

These words undoubtedly refer to Antiochus Epiphanes, who was the eighth king in the Seleucian dynasty. He came to power in 175 B.C. after murdering his brother, the rightful recipient of the throne. Antiochus was determined to unify his kingdom religiously and socially under the influence of Greek culture and idolatry. His attempt "led to a brutal suppression of Jewish worship at Jerusalem and generally throughout Palestine."[6] Antiochus's oppressive policies came to a head in December 168. At that time,

> he sent his general, Apollonius, with twenty thousand troops under orders to seize Jerusalem on the Sabbath. There he erected an idol of Zeus and desecrated the altar by offering swine on it. This idol became

---

5. Archer, "Daniel," p. 98.
6. Archer, "Daniel," p. 98.

known to the Jews as "the abomination of desolation" . . . , which served as a type of a future abomination that will be set up in the Jerusalem sanctuary to be built in the last days (cf. Christ's prediction in Matt. 24:15).[7]

During this siege, Antiochus killed a multitude of Jews and forbade them to practice their faith. He even threatened them with capital punishment if they attempted to circumcise their male children. On December 16, 167, he commanded the Jews "to offer unclean sacrifices and to eat swine's flesh or be penalized by death."[8] What's more, Antiochus made "the possession of the Hebrew Scriptures a capital offense" and minted coins that "actually bore the title *theos epiphanēs* ('God manifest')."[9] Given these blasphemous actions, it is little wonder that the Jews renamed Antiochus *Epiphanes*, which means "the Manifest or Illustrious One," calling him Antiochus *Epimanes*— "the Madman."[10] His reign of terror and acts of sacrilege did not last long, however. In 164, the eleventh year of his rule, Antiochus became seriously ill after hearing about the victories of Judas Maccabaeus, a Jew who sought to free his people from Antiochus's domination. Several days later, Antiochus died. And on December 14, 163, Judas Maccabaeus rededicated the Jerusalem temple to God and recommenced the daily sacrifices, "an event celebrated as Hanukkah by the Jewish community ever since."[11] The restoration of Israel's worship took place three years and fifty-five days after Antiochus's administrators had abolished the offering of sacrifices to the God of Israel.[12]

E. The future identity of the little horn. As we study Daniel 8:23–25, we discover that some of its descriptive phrases do not strictly apply to Antiochus Epiphanes. For example, the words " 'he will even oppose the Prince of princes' " (v. 25b) indicates the blatant opposition to Jesus Christ that will characterize the Antichrist (cf. Rev. 19:19) but could not have been true of Antiochus, since it was impossible for him to have known Jesus. Also, the comment " 'he will be broken without human agency' "

---

7. Archer, "Daniel," p. 98.

8. J. Dwight Pentecost, "Daniel," in *The Bible Knowledge Commentary: Old Testament Edition*, edited by John F. Walvoord and Roy B. Zuck (Wheaton, Ill.: Victor Books, 1985), p. 1358.

9. Archer, "Daniel," p. 104.

10. Pentecost, "Daniel," p. 1358.

11. Archer, "Daniel," p. 100.

12. Archer, "Daniel," p. 103.

(Dan. 8:25b) strongly suggests a judgment that was carried out by God Himself, instead of by natural means. We know from Scripture that such a supernatural judgment will fall on the Antichrist after Christ defeats him at the end of the Great Tribulation (Rev. 19:19–20). Therefore, from this incredible prophecy concerning Antiochus, we can learn several facts about the forthcoming Antichrist. Bible expositor J. Dwight Pentecost summarizes them for us this way:

> (1) He will achieve great power by subduing others [Dan. 8:24]. (2) He will rise to power by promising false security (v. 25). (3) He will be intelligent and persuasive (v. 23). (4) He will be controlled by another (v. 24), that is, Satan. (5) He will be an adversary of Israel and subjugate Israel to his authority (vv. 24–25). (6) He will rise up in opposition to the Prince of princes, the Lord Jesus Christ (v. 25). (7) His rule will be terminated by divine judgment (v. 25). So it may be concluded that there is a dual reference in this striking prophecy. It reveals Israel's history under the Seleucids and particularly under Antiochus during the time of Greek domination, but it also looks forward to Israel's experiences under Antichrist, whom Antiochus foreshadows.[13]

III. The Reaction

Following the conclusion of the vision, Daniel "was exhausted and sick for days" (Dan. 8:27a). After all, he had just received an amazing and terrifying look into the future, witnessing events that promised his fellow Jewish countrymen affliction more terrible than they had ever experienced. Even after he felt better and had resumed his governmental responsibilities, he was still "astounded at the vision" and unable to find anyone to give him further explanation (v. 27b). Because history has given us a clearer understanding of Daniel's vision than he had, our response to it may be be somewhat different than his was. Here are some reactions that might arise.

A. Initially, we may gain confidence in God's written Word. Practically all of this prophecy has been fulfilled, down to its most minute detail. This gives us reassurance that the rest of the Scriptures are true and reliable as well.

B. Eventually, we could become fearful. Anticipating the possibility of experiencing the dictatorial reign of a person like Antiochus Epiphanes could cause us to become extremely

---

13. Pentecost, "Daniel," p. 1359.

anxious. But if we are trusting in Christ as our Savior, we need not be afraid. For He has promised that He will protect us from the Antichrist by removing us from the face of the earth before he rises to power (Rev. 3:10; cf. 1 Thess. 4:13–18).[14] Therefore, we do not have to fear the coming of the Antichrist.

C. Hopefully, we will share with others the promise of salvation. It is one thing to find personal peace in our salvation through Christ. It is quite another to reach out and offer His deliverance to those who are living without hope. No one except God the Father knows when the Rapture of the Church will occur and the Great Tribulation will begin. But we know that these events will usher in terrible days of divine judgment for unbelievers. Out of compassion, we who are Christians should testify to others that God's wrath will only be escaped by those who place their faith in His Son, the Lord Jesus Christ. Will you begin sharing with non-Christians today?

Continued on next page

14. See the comments on Revelation 3:10 in the lesson titled "The Final World Dictator," p. 69.

A Comparison of Daniel 2, 7, and 8			
Daniel 2 Metals	Daniel 7 Animals	Daniel 8 Animals	Nations Represented
Gold	Winged Lion	—	Babylonia
Silver	Bear	Two-horned Ram	Medo-Persia
Bronze	Winged Leopard	Single-horned Goat	Greece
Iron, Iron and Clay	Ten-horned Beast	—	Rome, The Western Nations

This chart is a revised version of the one found in J. Dwight Pentecost's commentary, "Daniel," in *The Bible Knowledge Commentary: Old Testament Edition*, edited by John F. Walvoord and Roy B. Zuck (Wheaton, Ill.: Victor Books, 1985). p. 1356. Reprinted by permission.

🌳 *Living Insights*

Study One ━━━━━━━━━━━━━━━━━━━━━━━━━━━━━━━━━━━━

Some of what we read about in Daniel 8 is still to come, but many of the events prophesied in that chapter are now history. Hopefully, this lesson has heightened your curiosity concerning the history of Medo-Persia, Greece, Alexander the Great, and Antiochus Epiphanes.

* If you can gain access to a Bible encyclopedia, such as *The Zondervan Pictorial Encyclopedia of the Bible* or *The International Standard Bible Encyclopedia,* do some reading on the following subjects:
  —Media
  —Persia
  —Greece
  —Alexander the Great
  —Antiochus Epiphanes
  If you are unable to locate a Bible encyclopedia, make a trip to the public library and research these subjects in a standard resource work, such as *World Book Encyclopedia* or *Encyclopedia Britannica.* What you discover will enhance your understanding of and appreciation for God's infallible Word.

🌳 *Living Insights*

Study Two ━━━━━━━━━━━━━━━━━━━━━━━━━━━━━━━━━━━━

Now that we have had an opportunity to study some history, a little evaluation is in order. History is a tremendous teacher, so let's reflect on what we have learned by answering the following questions:
—What historical fact was most outstanding to me?
—What impressed me about the Medes?
—What impressed me about the Persians?
—What impressed me about the Greeks?
—In what specific ways was I able to relate to Alexander the Great?
—How can the information I have found positively influence my pursuit of godliness?
—How can these discoveries help me develop more purposeful relationships with other people and with God?

True Confessions
Daniel 9:1–19

Throughout our study, we have examined several sweeping, profound, and detailed prophecies that have revealed much about history, but little about Daniel. In this lesson, however, the focus temporarily changes. Here we will find Daniel falling on his knees and praying. Of course, this is not the first time we have seen him turn to God in prayer (Dan. 2:17–18). In fact, we have learned that communion with God was a regular part of Daniel's life (6:10). But chapter 9 of the Book of Daniel contains our only opportunity to enter this man's private world and hear the content of one of his talks with God. What we will discover is Daniel's unguarded prayer of confession and petition on behalf of the Jewish people. As we examine his intercessory plea for divine forgiveness and restoration, let's take time to reflect on our own prayer life as well.

I. The Setting for His Prayer

The prayer recorded in Daniel 9 was offered "in the first year of Darius the son of Ahasuerus, of Median descent, who was made king over the kingdom of the Chaldeans" (v. 1). This dates it back to 538 B.C., just after the Babylonians' fall to the Medo-Persian military. Daniel was in his mid-eighties at this time and was serving under Darius as a commissioner—one of the highest civic posts in the Medo-Persian Empire (cf. 6:1–2). During the first year of this new government, Daniel was reading what the Lord had revealed to "Jeremiah the prophet [concerning] the completion of the desolations of Jerusalem" (9:2). He found that around 605 B.C., God had declared through Jeremiah that King Nebuchadnezzar would bring the Jews under Babylonian rule for seventy years as punishment for their disobedience to the Lord (Jer. 25:1–11). He also realized that this period of captivity had begun later the same year with Nebuchadnezzar's siege of Jerusalem. A result of this siege had been the exile of Daniel and many other Jews to Babylon. While rereading Jeremiah's prophecy, Daniel was reminded that his people's period of captivity was coming to an end. This discovery sent Daniel to his knees in prayer for the Jews.

> ### Personal Application
> As busy as Daniel must have been, he habitually found time to read God's Word and pray. He did not allow his demanding governmental responsibilities to crowd out daily meetings with the Lord. How is your alone time with God? Is it short and sporadic? Are you allowing "the tyranny of the urgent" to dethrone Him as the top priority in your life? Remember,

> prayer and the study of the Scriptures are essential for developing and maintaining a vital Christian walk.

II. The Ingredients of His Prayer

We learn that Daniel "gave [his] attention to the Lord God to seek Him by prayer and supplications, with fasting, sackcloth, and ashes," and to confess the sin of his people (Dan. 9:3–5). As we can see, the prophet's prayer time contained five important ingredients.

A. Concentration. Daniel focused his mind and energy on seeking God through prayer. He did not permit the pressures of the day to divert his attention from the Lord.

B. Supplication. The Hebrew term for *supplications* means "entreaties, pleadings." It conveys the idea of a servant earnestly requesting his king to meet particular needs. Daniel implored his Heavenly Master to hear his requests and fill them according to the promises in Scripture.

C. Fasting. John C. Whitcomb explains that "in the Bible, fasting was never a means to gain God's attention or to impress Him (Isa. 58:3–12; Zech. 7:5). It was a practical means of setting aside the time-consuming task of meal preparation in order to concentrate on the Lord Himself."[1] Daniel obviously believed that taking time to talk with God was more important than eating every meal. As Jesus said, " 'Man shall not live on bread alone, but on every word that proceeds out of the mouth of God' " (Matt. 4:4).

D. Humility. When an Old Testament believer wanted to manifest a profound "humbling of the soul before God in repentance and mortification on account of [his] sin and the punishment with which it had been visited, it was not unusual to put on sackcloth, rend the garments, and scatter ashes over the head (II Sam. 13:19; I Kings 21:27; I Macc. 3:47; Lam. 2:10; Jonah 3:5 . . .)."[2] By seeking the Lord with sackcloth and ashes, Daniel was overtly expressing both his deep sorrow for the Israelites' sin and their total dependence on God for forgiveness and restoration.

E. Honesty. Daniel did not try to conceal anything from the all-knowing Lord. Rather, he confessed his wrongdoing and that of his people, calling on God to exercise compassion on them and rescue them from their plight.

---

1. John C. Whitcomb, Jr., *Daniel*, Everyman's Bible Commentary (Chicago: Moody Press, 1985), p. 123.

2. Merrill F. Unger, "Fasting," in *Unger's Bible Dictionary*, 3d ed., rev. (Chicago: Moody Press, 1966), p. 345.

┌─ *Personal Application* ─────────────────────┐

The characteristics of Daniel's prayer provide criteria by
which you can evaluate your prayer life. Are you as
disciplined and fervent in your prayer life as Daniel was
in his? Do you come before God as a demanding tyrant,
or as a humble servant? Do you make your own needs the
center of your petitions, or do you intercede for others on
a regular basis? Are you honest about your desires and
needs when speaking to the Lord? Do you occasionally
break free from the daily routines of life in order to spend
extra moments with God? Is your prayer time invigorating
and fresh, or mundane and stale?
└──┘

III. The Content of His Prayer

Daniel's prayer contains worship, confession, and petition. Let's
briefly examine each of these aspects.

A. Worship. Daniel begins and interweaves his prayer with
acknowledgments of God's perfect character. He says that the
Lord is " 'great and awesome' " (Dan. 9:4a; cf. v. 15a). He also
expresses his respect for God's faithful and righteous dealings
with His people (vv. 4b, 12, 14, 16a). Furthermore, the prophet
recognizes that the Lord is a holy Judge, who cannot let
rebellion go undisciplined (vv. 12–14). Finally, he acknowledges
that the Lord is compassionate and forgiving, and that He will
not permit His people to be afflicted forever (vv. 4c, 9, 15a, 18–19).

B. Confession. With this understanding of God, it is little wonder
that Daniel opens his heart and confesses his sin before the
Lord. The essence of his confession is found in verses 5 and 6:

"We have sinned [i.e., missed the mark], committed
iniquity [i.e., engaged in distorted and crooked
conduct], acted wickedly [i.e., disturbed peace], and
rebelled [i.e., revolted and attacked], even turning
aside from Thy commandments and ordinances.
Moreover, we have not listened to Thy servants the
prophets, who spoke in Thy name to our kings, our
princes, our fathers, and all the people of the land."

C. Petition. After acknowledging his own wrongs and those of
his fellow countrymen, Daniel urges the Lord to fulfill His
promise to end the seventy years of Babylonian captivity
(vv. 16–19). His petition is one of fervency, as these words bear
out:

"O my God, incline Thine ear and hear! Open Thine
eyes and see our desolations and the city which is
called by Thy name; for we are not presenting our

supplications before Thee on account of any merits of our own, but on account of Thy great compassion. O Lord, hear! O Lord, forgive! O Lord, listen and take action! For Thine own sake, O my God, do not delay, because Thy city and Thy people are called by Thy name." (vv. 18–19)

Personal Application

Daniel's prayer manifests an attitude of humility coupled with a boldness in approach. His example shows us that the saint who advances on his knees will never have to retreat. Indeed, the New Testament encourages believers to approach God with confidence, expecting Him to respond in accordance with His perfect will (Matt. 7:7–11; John 14:13–14, 15:7; Eph. 3:12; Heb. 10:19–22). Do you seek God out, believing that He will grant your requests? Furthermore, do you bring more than petitions to Him? Daniel not only made requests; he also confessed wrongdoing and gave honor to the Lord. To help you maintain a vital relationship with God through prayer, we have provided a chart at the end of this lesson that mentions five categories of prayer. We encourage you to study these facets on your own and employ them in your communications with the Lord.

IV. The Motive behind His Prayer

Daniel acknowledged that there was nothing he or his fellow Jews could do to earn God's forgiveness. Rather, the answer to his prayer depended solely on the Lord's superabundant compassion (Dan. 9:18b). We should also observe that Daniel's primary passion was not for himself or the other Jews, but for God's glory. Daniel called on the Lord to restore Israel and Jerusalem for His sake, not anyone else's (vv. 17b, 19b). This Hebrew prophet was concerned that the Lord's reputation would be marred if He did not free His people from captivity and return them to their native soil as He had promised.

Personal Application

Do your prayers reflect selfish interests, or divine values? Do you intercede on behalf of your national and local leaders? Do you ask the Lord to use you and others to glorify His name in your neighborhood, city, or country? Are you concerned with upholding God's character in all that you think, say, and do? Only when you focus your eyes on the Lord will you and your nation experience the many benefits of prayer.

Prayer

Categories	Explanations	Scriptures
Worship, or Praise	Expressing worth, adoration, and honor to God	1 Chronicles 29:11–13 Psalm 146:1–2 Romans 11:33 Revelation 4:10–11, 5:12–14
Confession	Declaring openly and honestly our disobedience; claiming God's forgiveness through the merits of Christ	Psalms 32:5, 38:18, 51:1–3, 66:18 Proverbs 28:13 1 John 1:9
Thanksgiving	Acknowledging our gratitude to God for His blessings and provisions as well as His tests and discipline	Psalm 103:1–5 Romans 1:8 Ephesians 5:20 1 Thessalonians 5:18
Intercession	Supporting others in prayer . . . remembering their special needs	1 Samuel 12:23 Ephesians 1:18 1 Timothy 2:1–2 James 5:14–16
Petition	Expressing our own needs and requests to God	Philippians 4:6–7 1 Thessalonians 5:17 Hebrews 4:14–16 James 1:5–8

Living Insights

Study One ▬▬▬▬▬▬▬▬▬▬▬▬▬▬▬▬▬▬▬▬▬▬▬▬▬▬▬▬▬▬▬▬▬▬▬▬▬▬

The Scriptures include at least five distinct categories of prayer—all of which should be expressions of a Christian's devotion to God. Let's research some of the biblical texts that describe them.

- At the end of this lesson was a chart that listed the five aspects of prayer, along with Scripture references that support each of them. As you carefully read through the passages, record your observations, feelings, and impressions on a page in your notebook. Some of the texts may be familiar; others may be new to you. Ask God to use this exercise to give you some new insight on prayer.

Living Insights

Study Two ▬▬▬▬▬▬▬▬▬▬▬▬▬▬▬▬▬▬▬▬▬▬▬▬▬▬▬▬▬▬▬▬▬▬▬▬▬

Our times of prayer should be fresh and alive. Perhaps employing the guidelines mentioned in the chart will open new avenues for creativity in our communication with God.

- Once again, return to the chart that was found at the end of this lesson. Experiment by patterning a prayer of your own after the suggestions in the chart. Take five minutes for worship; then five more minutes for confession; and so on, until you have engaged in each facet of prayer. At the conclusion of the twenty-five minutes, take a few moments to evaluate this prayer time. Was it helpful? Did you include elements of prayer that you had been neglecting? Was it awkward for you in certain categories? If so, why? You may want to return to this chart occasionally and use it to add new spark to your alone times with God.

The Backbone of Biblical Prophecy

Daniel 9:24–27

The vision of the seventy weeks revealed in Daniel 9 is undoubtedly the backbone of prophecy concerning Israel, Christ, and the Antichrist. It is also true that fewer predictions in Scripture have been interpreted in as many ways as have the seventy weeks of Daniel.[1] Given this fact, we will make every attempt to allow the Bible to speak for itself as we apply to this chapter the rules of literary interpretation. Let's not delay our exploration of this passage any further, for what awaits us is the excitement of unlocking one of the most incredible prophecies recorded anywhere in God's Word.

I. Some Important Background

We should recall from the last lesson that the ninth chapter of the Book of Daniel contains a prayer offered by the prophet Daniel "in the first year of Darius" (9:1), which was around 538 B.C. Sometime during that year, Daniel observed in the writings of Jeremiah that the predicted seventy-year captivity of the Jews was nearing completion (v. 2; cf. Jer. 25:3–11, 29:10–14). So he came before God on his knees, pleading with the Lord to forgive the sins of the Jews and allow them to return to their native land and rebuild Jerusalem (Dan. 9:4–19). While Daniel was still praying, he was revisited by the angel Gabriel (vv. 20–21; cf. 8:16–17). Appearing in human form, Gabriel told the elderly prophet that he had been sent to give him " 'insight with understanding' " (v. 22b). To this the angel added, " 'At the beginning of your supplications the command was issued, and I have come to tell you, for you are highly esteemed; so give heed to the message and gain understanding of the vision' " (v. 23). Apparently, Gabriel had been sent by God with the answer to Daniel's fervent prayer. However, we will see that the answer Gabriel revealed transcended Daniel's prayer request, unveiling events that would transpire centuries after the reconstruction of Jerusalem.

II. The Seventy Weeks

Daniel 9:24–27 records God's response to Daniel's petition. Read these verses a few times before continuing in the lesson:

> "Seventy weeks have been decreed for your people and
> your holy city, to finish the transgression, to make an end
> of sin, to make atonement for iniquity, to bring in
> everlasting righteousness, to seal up vision and prophecy,

---

1. Here are two sources that give many of these interpretations: J. Barton Payne, *Encyclopedia of Biblical Prophecy: The Complete Guide to Scriptural Predictions and Their Fulfillment* (New York: Harper and Row, 1973), pp. 384–85; Louis E. Knowles, "The Interpretation of the Seventy Weeks of Daniel in the Early Fathers," *The Westminster Theological Journal* 7:2 (May 1945), pp. 136–60.

and to anoint the most holy place. So you are to know and discern that from the issuing of a decree to restore and rebuild Jerusalem until Messiah the Prince there will be seven weeks and sixty-two weeks; it will be built again, with plaza and moat, even in times of distress. Then after the sixty-two weeks the Messiah will be cut off and have nothing, and the people of the prince who is to come will destroy the city and the sanctuary. And its end will come with a flood; even to the end there will be war; desolations are determined. And he will make a firm covenant with the many for one week, but in the middle of the week he will put a stop to sacrifice and grain offering; and on the wing of abominations will come one who makes desolate, even until a complete destruction, one that is decreed, is poured out on the one who makes desolate."

Before we deal with this passage in detail, let's make some general observations about it. First, the text informs us that *a specific period of time has been marked out by God*—namely, seventy weeks. Second, we learn that this prophecy is *directly related to the Jews and Jerusalem.* Gabriel tells the Hebrew prophet, " 'Seventy weeks have been decreed for your people and your holy city' " (v. 24a). Thus, the predictions given are designed for Israel, not the Church. And third, we are told that *the events prophesied will occur during this seventy-week period that has been divided into three segments.* The first division is seven weeks long, the second is sixty-two weeks, and the third is one week. With these facts in mind, let's probe the depths of this vision.

A. The meaning of the phrase "seventy weeks." Throughout this prophecy, the Hebrew term translated *weeks* literally means "units of seven." Of course, the question is, To what do the units of seven refer? The overwhelming consensus among Bible scholars is that the units of seven designate years, not days or weeks.[2] In this case, the seventy units of seven would equal 490 years. There are several good reasons for adopting this understanding. For instance, since Daniel had been praying in reference to the seventy years of Jewish captivity brought about by divine judgment (v. 2), it would have been natural for him to have understood these seventy sevens as years. In regard to this, J. Dwight Pentecost makes these insightful observations:

2. Michael J. Gruenthaner even goes so far as to say, "All critics are agreed that the seventy weeks cannot be ordinary weeks but must be seventy periods of seven years each. For it is impossible to find any epoch in Jewish history, lasting but 490 days, in which the events narrated could possibly be verified" ("The Seventy Weeks," *The Catholic Biblical Quarterly* 1[1939], p. 47).

"Whereas people today think in units of ten (e.g., decades), Daniel's people thought in terms of sevens....Seven days are in one week. Every seventh year was a sabbath rest year (Lev. 25:1–7). Seven 'sevens' brought them to the Year of Jubilee (Lev. 25:8–12)."[3] Furthermore, part of the reason the Jews served seventy years in exile was that they willfully failed to observe the sabbatical years over a 490-year period (2 Chron. 36:20–21; cf. Lev. 26:32–35, 40–45). The Mosaic Law clearly specified that the Jews were to leave the land in Israel uncultivated every seventh year (Lev. 25:1–7). Because the Jews had violated this command, they spent one year in captivity for every Sabbath year they had not kept.[4] With this in mind, we can be fairly certain Daniel understood the seventy units of seven decreed for Israel's future in light of the 490 years of exile that had been the result of Israel's past disobedience. Moreover, as Dwight Pentecost further explains, the seventy sevens in Daniel's prophecy "could not designate *days* (about 1⅓ years) for that would not be enough time for the events in Daniel 9:24–27 to occur. The same is true of 490 weeks of seven days each (i.e., 3,430 days, about 9½ years)."[5] And finally, "if days were intended one would expect Daniel to have added 'of days' after '70 sevens' for in 10:2–3 he wrote literally, 'three sevens of days' "[6]—that is, three weeks. Therefore, it seems clear that the "seventy weeks" in Daniel 9 should be understood as seventy seven-year periods, which collectively equal 490 years.

B. The six objectives to be accomplished. During this 490-year time span, six aims are to be achieved. The first three have to do with sin, and the last three are concerned with the Millennial Kingdom. Let's briefly look at each one. The first objective mentioned is the finishing of transgression (9:24a). Jesus Christ paid the penalty for man's sin on the cross at Calvary, but human beings still commit wrongs. Therefore, the persistence of sin needs to be dealt with; and it will be, particularly in relationship to Israel when she finally repents and acknowledges Christ as her Savior prior to His Second Advent. The second goal is " 'to make an end of sin' " (v. 24b)—

3. J. Dwight Pentecost, "Daniel," in *The Bible Knowledge Commentary: Old Testament Edition*, edited by John F. Walvoord and Roy B. Zuck (Wheaton, Ill.: Victor Books, 1985), p. 1361.

4. See Harold W. Hoehner, *Chronological Aspects of the Life of Christ* (Grand Rapids, Mich.: Zondervan Publishing House, 1977), pp. 117–18; Robert C. Newman, "Daniel's Seventy Weeks and the Old Testament Sabbath-Year Cycle," *Journal of the Evangelical Theological Society* 16:4 (Fall 1973), p. 231.

5. Pentecost, "Daniel," p. 1361.

6. Pentecost, "Daniel," p. 1361.

that is, to seal up disobedience with a view to punish and remove it (cf. Deut. 32:32–35, Job 14:16–17). In regard to Israel, the foundation for this being accomplished was laid when Christ bore the punishment for the sins of the world. But Israel's sin will not be totally removed from her until the Lord returns to earth and establishes His Kingdom (Ezek. 37:21–27, Rom. 11:25–27). The third objective is the " '[making of] atonement for iniquity' " (Dan. 9:24b). Once again, the basic provision for the reconciliation of man to God was made at Calvary. However, as far as Israel is concerned, the actual application of Christ's death is associated with the Second Coming. The fourth goal, " '[bringing] in everlasting righteousness,' " will be fulfilled in the Millennial Kingdom (v. 24c; cf. Isa. 60:21, Jer. 23:5–6). The fifth objective is " 'to seal up vision and prophecy' " (Dan. 9:24d). John C. Whitcomb explains it well:

> In the postapostolic phase of church history, we have no further need of such ministries, possessing as we do the completed revelation of God in Holy Scripture. [However] during the first half of the seventieth week of Daniel two witnesses will prophesy to Israel in order to launch the 144,000 [saved Jews] and others into a global witness for Christ after the rapture of the church (Rev. 11:3–12). But all such prophetic ministries will end forever at our Lord's return to earth.[7]

The last goal mentioned is the " '[anointing of] the most holy place' " (Dan. 9:24d). This may be referring to the dedication of the holy of holies in the millennial temple, as described in Ezekiel 41–46. Or it could be denoting the enthronement of Christ as the King of kings in the Millennium.[8] Whichever the case, this objective is yet unfulfilled.

C. The three divisions. As noted earlier, the seventy sets of seven years are divided into three distinct periods. *The first division comprised seven units of seven, or forty-nine years.* The beginning of this period was to be marked by " 'the issuing of a decree to restore and rebuild Jerusalem' " (Dan. 9:25a). The text adds that the city would be " 'built again, with plaza and moat, even in times of distress' " (v. 25c). Various suggestions have been made regarding which decree in history fulfilled this part of the prophecy. However, only one decree granting

7. John C. Whitcomb, *Daniel,* Everyman's Bible Commentary (Chicago: Moody Press, 1985), p. 130.

8. See Pentecost, "Daniel," p. 1362; Whitcomb, *Daniel,* p. 131; John F. Walvoord, *Daniel: The Key to Prophetic Revelation* (Chicago: Moody Press, 1971), p. 223.

permission and supplies for the rebuilding of Jerusalem was ever made to the Jews, and that was the one given by the Persian king Artaxerxes I to Nehemiah in March or April of 445/444 B.C. (Neh. 2:1–8).[9] Nehemiah even records that the restoration of Jerusalem's walls was carried out under trying conditions (vv. 17–19, 4:1–6:19), just as Daniel had predicted. However, the rebuilding of the entire city was not completed until 396 B.C., forty-nine years after Artaxerxes I issued his decree. *The second major division was to last 434 years,* ending in A.D. 37/38, approximately five years *after* Christ's crucifixion. This speculation conflicts with the prediction in Daniel 9:26 that the Messiah would die after the 483-year period came to an end. However, a resolution for this issue can be found by understanding that, in Daniel's day, the Jewish calendar measured time by 360-day—or *lunar*—years, rather than by 365-day—or *solar*—years, the standard measurement in most contemporary cultures.[10] Using lunar years as the standard for computation, we find that a 483-year period is 173,880 days. After making some minor adjustments due to the Jewish practice of occasionally adding a month to correct the calendar, we arrive at March or April of A.D. 32/33. New Testament scholar Harold Hoehner calculates that the end of the 483 years occurred on March 30 in A.D. 33—the same date he concludes Jesus Christ entered Jerusalem as the King of the Jews (Luke 19:36–40, John 12:12–15; cf. Zech. 9:9). If this scholar's calculations are correct, Christ was crucified, or " 'cut off,' " four days later—just after the end of the sixty-ninth week and exactly as predicted in Daniel 9:26a.[11] Between the completion of the first 483 years of Daniel's prophecy and the last seven years, some other events are predicted. One such event will occur when " 'the people of the prince who is to come will destroy the city and the sanctuary. And its end will come with a flood' " (v. 26b). This part of the prophecy was literally fulfilled in A.D. 70, when a Roman general named Titus forced his way into Jerusalem. On August 6 of that year, his troops burned the temple and leveled it. They also destroyed the city and its fortifications, just as both Daniel and

9. For more discussion on this point, see: Walvoord, *Daniel,* pp. 224–27; Hoehner, *Chronological Aspects,* pp. 119–28.

10. The reasoning for computing the seventy weeks according to a lunar year rather than a solar year is provided in these sources: Hoehner, *Chronological Aspects,* pp. 133–37; Sir Robert Anderson, *The Coming Prince* (Grand Rapids, Mich.: Kregel Publications, 1957), chap. 6; Alva J. McClain, *Daniel's Prophecy of the Seventy Weeks* (Grand Rapids, Mich.: Zondervan Publishing House, 1940), pp. 15–17.

11. See Hoehner, *Chronological Aspects,* pp. 137–39.

Christ had predicted (v. 26b, Luke 19:41–44). Following this terrible destruction, Daniel 9:26c states that " 'even to the end there will be war; desolations are determined' " (cf. Matt. 24:6–8; Luke 21:20–24). Of course, history has amply verified the fulfillment of this prediction. Then, after an indeterminate length of time, *the third major division of Daniel's prophecy will begin —namely, the one unit of seven, or the final seven years.* Toward the beginning of this period, " 'he [i.e., the Antichrist] will make a firm covenant with the many for one week, but in the middle of the week he will put a stop to sacrifice and grain offering' " (Dan. 9:27a). Apparently, the Antichrist will make a covenant with Israel, permitting her to offer sacrifices in the restored temple of Jerusalem. However, in the middle of this seven-year period, the Antichrist will break the covenant and stop all temple sacrifices to the God of Israel. At that time, this wicked ruler will establish his own religion and command the world to worship him (cf. 2 Thess. 2:3–4; Rev. 13:7–8, 12). As awful as this period of abominations of desolation will be (Matt. 24:15–22), it will not extend past the seven-year period specified in the Book of Daniel. The Antichrist, who will seek to destroy the Lord and His people, will fall under the wrath of God (Dan. 9:27b) and be "thrown alive into the lake of fire which burns with brimstone" (Rev. 19:20b). This will both mark the end of the events detailed in the 490 years of Daniel 9:25–27 and lead to the beginning of the Millennial Kingdom briefly described in 9:24b.

III. Some Relevant Application

The information Gabriel revealed to Daniel is truly remarkable. Much of it has already come to pass—accurate to the last detail. This assures us that what remains to be fulfilled will be brought about according to God's perfect timetable. Reflecting on the matters we have studied in this lesson, we can draw at least two truths that are applicable to our lives.

A. God deals in specifics. When Daniel made a specific request in prayer, the Lord answered with particulars, not generalities. This should encourage us to make our requests as specific as possible.

B. God keeps His promises. The events predicted in the seventy weeks that have occurred so far have happened just as God said they would. This should give us confidence that the Lord will keep all the promises He has given in His written Word.

The Seventy Weeks of Daniel

Artaxerxes I's Decree to Restore Jerusalem	Restoration Completed	Christ's Triumphal Entry	Jerusalem and the Temple Destroyed	Antichrist Makes a Covenant with Israel	Antichrist Breaks the Covenant	Antichrist Defeated by Christ

Christ Cut Off after 69th Week

War and Desolation to the End

7 Weeks (49 Years)	62 Weeks (434 Years)	Church Age	1 Week

(3½ Years) (3½ Years)

445 / 444 B.C.	396 B.C.	A.D. 32 / 33	A.D. 70	A.D. ?	A.D. ?	A.D. ?

🌱 *Living Insights*

Study One ▬▬▬▬▬▬▬▬▬▬▬▬▬▬▬▬▬▬▬▬▬▬▬

As the title of this lesson states, Daniel 9:24–27 is the backbone of biblical prophecy. The first sixty-nine weeks of this prediction have already taken place. It is the seventieth week that has yet to be fulfilled.

● Let's read the words of Christ concerning the final week. Copy this chart into your notebook. Then read Matthew 24 and write down the phrases that describe this seven-year period of judgment and destruction.

Daniel's Seventieth Week—Matthew 24	
Verses	Descriptions

🌱 *Living Insights*

Study Two ▬▬▬▬▬▬▬▬▬▬▬▬▬▬▬▬▬▬▬▬▬▬▬

That final week in Daniel's prophecy predicts some pretty scary stuff! But we who know Christ are not like those "who have no hope" (1 Thess. 4:13b). We have His promise that we will not experience the events of the seventieth week.

● Let's spend some time meditating on 1 Thessalonians 4:13–5:11. This passage speaks about the Rapture and the Tribulation, and it was written to comfort and encourage believers concerning their involvement with, as well as their response to, these events. Read this section of Scripture slowly and reflectively. Then give thanks to God for His protection, His mercy, His love.

Demons between Heaven and Earth

Daniel 10

Interest in the occult and paranormal phenomena is on the rise today. The movie industry has certainly capitalized on this heightened curiosity, not to mention the numerous television programs, newspaper columns, magazine articles, game manufacturers, and book publishers that have hyped these topics as well. Unfortunately, the fragments of truth that are sometimes communicated about the demonic world are frequently lost amidst sensational stories and exaggerated remarks. Consequently, many people have a distorted understanding of the satanic realm. The teaching of Scripture on this subject stands in stark contrast to the misinformation that is commonly perpetuated and consumed. Some of the biblical data about demons is found in Daniel 10. Among other things, this passage exposes the unseen war being waged against God's people by demonic forces. And, thankfully, this chapter makes it clear that those who fight on the Lord's side have the power they need to overcome the Adversary (cf. Eph. 6:10–18; 1 John 4:3–4, 5:4–5, 18). So let's take this opportunity to gain a biblical perspective on the invisible war being fought in between heaven and earth.

I. The Period and the Prophet

The events recorded in Daniel 10 took place in "the third year of Cyrus king of Persia" (v. 1). This would have been in 335 or 334 B.C., since Darius the Mede—otherwise known as Gubaru—reigned over the former Babylonian Empire as Cyrus's viceroy until 338 or 337.[1] If Daniel was born around 620, he would have been in his mid-eighties during this period. Furthermore, we know that Cyrus, during his first official year as king, gave the Jewish exiles permission to return to Jerusalem and rebuild the temple (Ezra 1:1–4). Daniel did not go with this first group of captives, probably because he was too old to handle the rigors of travel. In addition, he was likely to have been more help to his departing Jewish brethren by remaining in Babylon as a political influence than by going to Jerusalem to aid them in the actual reconstruction of the temple. While serving under Cyrus, Daniel received a message that foretold a "great conflict" involving the Jews and the nation of Israel (Dan. 10:1b). The prophet "understood the message" (v. 1c), and it apparently shook him up, for the text states that over a period of three weeks he mourned, fasted, and neglected personal grooming in order to petition God in prayer (vv. 2–3, 12).

1. See Gleason L. Archer, Jr., "Daniel," in *The Expositor's Bible Commentary,* 12 vols., edited by Frank E. Gaebelein (Grand Rapids, Mich.: Regency Reference Library, Zondervan Publishing House, 1976–), vol. 7, p. 122.

II. The Messenger and the Vision

As he was standing with some other men by the bank of the Tigris River, Daniel saw a vision of "a certain man dressed in linen, whose waist was girded with a belt of pure gold of Uphaz. His body also was like beryl, his face had the appearance of lightning, his eyes were like flaming torches, his arms and feet like the gleam of polished bronze, and the sound of his words like the sound of a tumult" (vv. 5–6; cf. Rev. 10:1–3). Daniel states that he alone was able to see this incredible-looking angel who appeared in human form (Dan. 10:7a). And although his companions did not witness the vision, "a great dread fell on them, and they ran away to hide themselves" (v. 7b). "So," Daniel writes, "I was left alone and saw this great vision; yet no strength was left in me, for my natural color turned to a deathly pallor, and I retained no strength" (v. 8). Emotionally overwhelmed, Daniel passed out and slumped to the ground as soon as he heard the angel speak (v. 9).

III. The Prayer and the Response

Daniel was awakened when the angel touched him, but he did not stand up. He rose to his hands and knees, still afraid of the awesome figure he was seeing (v. 10). Then the angel spoke again: " 'O Daniel, man of high esteem, understand the words that I am about to tell you and stand upright, for I have now been sent to you' " (v. 11a). Daniel obeyed the angelic messenger and rose to his feet, continuing to tremble (v. 11b). Embedded in the remainder of this story are five principles of prayer we should consider.

A. Believers' prayers are immediately heard by God. The messenger told Daniel, " 'Do not be afraid, . . . for from the first day that you set your heart on understanding this and on humbling yourself before your God, your words were heard, and I have come in response to your words' " (v. 12). Like Daniel, we have immediate access to God through prayer. However, as the next verse points out, we will not always receive prompt replies to our petitions.

B. Demonic forces can delay answers to prayer. Although the angel was dispatched right away to bring the answer to Daniel's request, he was kept from fulfilling his mission for three weeks because of the opposition he received from " 'the prince of the kingdom of Persia' " (v. 13a). This is a reference not to a human ruler but to a fallen angel who had been given authority by Satan to watch over the affairs related to the Medo-Persian Empire. We know from other passages that "the whole world lies in the power of the evil one" (1 John 5:19b; cf. John 12:31). Since this is so, it is understandable that Satan seeks to acquire dominance by assigning demonic agents to various parts of the globe in an attempt to thwart God's activity. And although it is true that satanic resistance does occasionally hinder the Lord's work, it does not indicate that God's power and sovereignty are less than ultimate. Gleason Archer makes this point clear:

> While God can, of course, override the united resistance of all the forces of hell if he chooses to do so, he accords to demons certain limited powers of obstruction and rebellion somewhat like those he allows humans. In both cases the exercise of free will in opposition to the Lord of heaven is permitted by him when he sees fit. But as Job 1:12 and 2:6 indicate, the malignity of Satan is never allowed to go beyond the due limit set by God, who will not allow the believer to be tested beyond his limit (1 Cor. 10:13).[2]

Daniel had been unaware of the spiritual conflict that had taken place in between heaven and earth as a result of his prayer. But he became informed that the angel who was delivering God's response had finally won the battle with the demon over Medo-Persia. This victory was made possible by the help of the angel " 'Michael, one of the chief princes' " of the Lord's heavenly messengers (Dan. 10:13b). Apparently, Michael had greater power than either the good angel or the wicked one. This eye-opening look into the invisible war being fought around us should cause us to pay heed to the exhortation in Ephesians 6:11–12: "Put on the full armor of God, that you may be able to stand firm against the schemes of the devil. For our struggle is not against flesh and blood, but against the rulers, against the powers, against the world forces of this darkness, against the spiritual forces of wickedness in the heavenly places."

C. Wrestling in prayer is exhausting work. After being told by the angelic messenger that the future of the Jews was about to be unveiled, Daniel "turned [his] face toward the ground and became speechless" (Dan. 10:14–15). Then, either the same angel or another one enabled Daniel to express how he felt (v. 16a)— how he was overcome with anguish, totally debilitated, and gasping for breath (vv. 16b–17). It is probable that these were the effects of both his anticipation of the revelation concerning Israel's future and the weakened state he was in due to the three weeks spent in fervent prayer. Daniel had engaged in spiritual warfare on his knees and, in doing so, had advanced God's cause on earth. He learned, however, that the spiritual battle believers wage can sometimes take a physical toll. Even so, we can readily see that fatigue is a small price to pay for curbing evil and furthering good.

2. Archer, "Daniel," p. 125.

D. Following wearisome times of prayer, strength returns in extra measures. The text tells us that the same angel who helped Daniel speak also gave him the strength to see the vision that was about to be revealed (vv. 18–19). In the Epistle to the Hebrews, we learn that angels are "ministering spirits [who are] sent out [by God] to render service for the sake of those who will inherit salvation [i.e., the Millenial Kingdom]" (Heb. 1:14; cf. 2:5, 9:28). Even Jesus Christ was strengthened by angels after going without food for forty days and being tempted by Satan in the wilderness (Matt. 4:11, Mark 1:13). Today, the Lord still uses His heavenly ministers to encourage us in our walk with Him and to protect us in our fight against satanic powers.

E. Overcoming demonic forces is not a once-and-for-all matter. The angel who brought God's answer to Daniel said he would be returning " 'to fight against the prince of Persia,' " who would be succeeded or aided by another demon called " 'the prince of Greece' " (Dan. 10:20). However, this angelic messenger assured Daniel that he would not leave until he had explained the vision to him (v. 21a). To this the angel added that only the angelic chief prince Michael could give him adequate support in his battle against demonic forces (v. 21b). The conflict between God and Satan is still being fought today. Christ's death on the cross has ensured Satan's defeat, but it has not yet ended the war (Heb. 2:14; 1 John 3:8; Rev. 12–13, 19:19–20:10). However, we who are Christians have God's promise that the ultimate victory over satanic powers is ours "because greater is He who is in [us] than he who is in the world" (1 John 4:4).

IV. Some Concluding Thoughts

In 2 Kings 6, we find a story that records an amazing incident in the life of another prophet—Elisha. This man of God was surrounded one night by a foreign army that had been sent to capture him (vv. 8–14). Elisha's servant saw this great military force when he went outside in the early morning hours (v. 15a). Struck by fear, he ran to Elisha and asked, " 'What shall we do?' " (v. 15b). The prophet's response displayed insight that his servant did not possess: " 'Do not fear, for those who are with us are more than those who are with them' " (v. 16). Then Elisha prayed that God would enable this servant to see the invisible (v. 17a). So "the Lord opened the servant's eyes, . . . [and] he saw . . . [that] the mountain was full of horses and chariots of fire all around Elisha" (v. 17b). This ancient story, like the encounter recorded in Daniel 10, surfaces at least two thoughts we would be wise to recall.

A. If we could see the invisible, we would be amazed at the presence of good and evil forces around us.

B. Even if we are not enabled to see the invisible, we should be encouraged by the invincible might of God within us.

 Living Insights

Overcoming demonic influence is not a once-and-for-all matter. It is a war that must be fought continually. To help us see this, let's examine some individuals' actual encounters with demonic attack recorded in the New Testament.

• The chart on the facing page lists some passages from Matthew, Mark, Luke, and Acts which discuss demons. The headings in the chart will help you organize your thoughts concerning this subject. In some of the accounts, you will not be able to discover all the information the chart calls for, but explore the passages as thoroughly as possible for answers. Use this Living Insights to work your way through the references cited in Matthew and Mark only.

 Living Insights

Luke, the writer of both the Gospel of Luke and the Acts of the Apostles, records nine separate incidents of demonic activity. Let's continue our study of spiritual warfare as we complete the chart we began in Study One.

	Demons in the New Testament				
Scriptures	Victims	Tormentors	Victims' Experiences	Methods Used to Expel Demons	Demons' Responses	Final Results
Matthew 4:24 8:16 8:28–33 9:32–33 12:22 15:22–28 17:14–20 **Mark** 1:23–27 3:10–11 16:9 **Luke** 6:17–18 7:21 11:14–26 13:10–17 **Acts** 5:16 8:7 13:6–11 16:16–18 19:11–16						

Wars and Rumors of War
Daniel 11:1–12:1

Shortly after the Fall of Adam and Eve, the first drops of human blood were vindictively shed (Gen. 4:3–8). And ever since, the path of man's history has been strewn with the victims of personal vendettas, national revolutions, and international wars. It seems that no matter how hard people try to put an end to human conflict, peace continues to elude their grasp. Why is this so? The Apostle James puts his finger on the reason. Observe what he says: "What is the source of quarrels and conflicts among you? Is not the source your pleasures that wage war in your members? You lust and do not have; so you commit murder. And you are envious and cannot obtain; so you fight and quarrel" (James 4:1–2a). *Selfishness*—that is the well from which springs personal, national, and worldwide strife. During the Tribulation, the final military campaign against the Lord will be an unmatched exhibition of man's sinfulness. The stage for this last battle will be set by other greed-oriented strife that will precede it. These events are described in the last two chapters of the Book of Daniel. As we begin our study of this portion of God's Word, we will be reminded that although self-centeredness presently seems to reign supreme, the Lord has consistently demonstrated His ultimate control over sin and, one day, He will confine selfishness to hell forever.

I. Some Ugly Wars of the Past

We should recall that the events described in Daniel 11–12 are part of the revelation that came to the prophet Daniel "in the third year of Cyrus king of Persia" (Dan. 10:1a). The human-like angel who spoke to Daniel unveiled some things that were to take place in human history. From our perspective, we can see that some of the events predicted have already been fulfilled. However, even those happenings that are now past foreshadow events that are still to come. By keeping this fact in mind, we will discover the full significance of what the angel presented to Daniel.

A. Conflicts under the Medo-Persian Empire.
The angelic messenger told Daniel that Cyrus would be succeeded by four more Medo-Persian kings, the fourth of whom would be wealthier and mightier than the others and would wage war against the Grecian Empire (11:2). We know from the annals of history that these rulers were Cambyses (530–522 B.C.), Gaumata (522), Darius I Hystaspes (521–486), and Xerxes (486–465)—the very rich and extremely powerful monarch referred to as King Ahasuerus throughout the Book of Esther. Xerxes did launch a "great campaign against Greece from 481 to 479, with an army of probably 200,000 men and a navy of many hundreds of ships

gathered from all over his vast empire."[1] John C. Whitcomb explains that "Xerxes desperately sought to avenge the humiliating defeat suffered by his father, Darius I, at [the hands of the Greeks during] the battle of Marathon (490). But his army was defeated north of Athens at Plataea (479), just after his navy was smashed at Salamis, to the west of Athens."[2]

B. Conflicts under the Grecian Empire. The Greek ruler who eventually conquered the Medo-Persian Empire was Alexander the Great. Although he had a short career (334–323), his military prowess brought him the authority to govern practically all of the then-known world (v. 3).

C. Conflicts between the Ptolemies and the Seleucids. Following Alexander's death, his kingdom was divided among four of his generals (v. 4): Cassander had control over Macedonia and Greece; Lysimachus governed Thrace and parts of Asia Minor; Ptolemy ruled over Egypt and Palestine; and Seleucus maintained sovereignty over northern Syria and Mesopotamia. None of these individuals were blood relatives of Alexander, nor were they appointed by him to rule over his empire (v. 4b). As Gleason Archer explains:

> The infant son of Alexander III (the Great) was Alexander IV, born of the Persian princess Roxana. Kept under Cassander's custody, he was removed by murder in 310 B.C. His uncle, Philip Arrhidaeus, who was an illegitimate brother of Alexander III and mentally deranged, had already been assassinated in 317. Thus there were no descendants ... to succeed Alexander himself, and the prediction "not go to his descendants" found fulfillment. The four ruthless and powerful generals named above became the "Diadochi" ("Successors") who engineered the partition of the Macedonian Empire into four realms.[3]

Daniel 11:5–35 discloses in detail the peace that " 'the king of the South' " and " 'the king of the North' " would try to establish and the wars they would wage against one another. From historical records we know that the first king of the South was Ptolemy I Soter of Egypt, founder of the Ptolemian dynasty, and

1. John C. Whitcomb, *Daniel*, Everyman's Bible Commentary (Chicago: Moody Press, 1985), p. 146.

2. Whitcomb, *Daniel*, p. 146.

3. Gleason L. Archer, Jr., "Daniel," in *The Expositor's Bible Commentary*, 12 vols., edited by Frank E. Gaebelein (Grand Rapids, Mich.: Regency Reference Library, Zondervan Publishing Co., 1976–   ), vol. 7, p. 129.

that the first monarch of the North was Seleucus I Nicator of Syria, the one who established the Seleucid dynasty. The following chart identifies the various rulers of each dynasty and their relationship to the eleventh chapter of the Book of Daniel.[4]

The Ptolemies and the Seleucids in Daniel 11:5–35			
Ptolemies (Kings "of the South," Egypt)		**Seleucids** (Kings "of the North," Syria)	
Daniel 11:5	Ptolemy I Soter (323–285 B.C.)*	Daniel 11:5	Seleucus I Nicator (312–281 B.C.)
11:6	Ptolemy II Philadelphus (285–246)		Antiochus I Soter† (281–262)
		11:6	Antiochus II Theos (262–246)
11:7–8	Ptolemy III Euergetes (246–221)	11:7–9	Seleucus II Callinicus (246–227)
		11:10	Seleucus III Soter (227–223)
11:11–12, 14–15	Ptolemy IV Philopator (221–204)	11:10–11, 13, 15–19	Antiochus III the Great (223–187)
11:17	Ptolemy V Epiphanes (204–181)		
		11:20	Seleucus IV Philopator (187–176)
11:25	Ptolemy VI Philometer (181–145)	11:21–32	Antiochus IV Epiphanes (175–163)

*The years designate the rulers' reigns.
†Not referred to in Daniel 11:5–35.

After referring to Seleucus I and his ascendancy over Ptolemy I (v. 5), the biblical account in verses 6–9 speaks of "the tragic marriage of Berenice, daughter of the king of the south, to the king of the north, . . . with some of its evil consequences (249–240 B.C.)."[5]

---

4. This chart appears on page 1367 in J. Dwight Pentecost's commentary titled "Daniel," in *The Bible Knowledge Commentary: Old Testament Edition*, edited by John F. Walvoord and Roy B. Zuck (Wheaton, Ill.: Victor Books, 1985). Reprinted by permission.

5. Whitcomb, *Daniel*, pp. 149–50.

The following section (vv. 10–19) leads up to the spectacular though tragic career of Antiochus III the Great (222–187 B.C.), including his defeat by Egypt at the Battle of Raphia (217 B.C.); his conquest of Palestine, "the glorious land" (198 B.C.); his catastrophic defeat by the Roman army at the Battle of Magnesia (190 B.C.) with the resulting loss of his claims to Greece and Asia Minor; the imposition of an enormous tribute upon him by Rome and the surrender of his son as a hostage (later Antiochus IV Epiphanes); and his death at Elymais.

Verse 20 speaks of the son of Antiochus III, Seleucus IV Philopater, who sent Hiliodorus to rob the Jerusalem Temple of its treasures and was then himself poisoned by Heliodorus.[6]

D. Conflicts under Antiochus Epiphanes. The man who foreshadows the coming Antichrist is the Syrian Seleucid king Antiochus IV Epiphanes (175–163 B.C.). His tyrannical and anti-Semitic career was prophesied by the angelic messenger who had been sent to Daniel to reveal the events we have discussed in this lesson so far. Looking back in history, we can confirm that the details of this prophecy were completely fulfilled. Antiochus illegally seized the Syrian throne from Seleucus IV, the son of his murdered brother (v. 21). Then Antiochus proceeded to secure his domain and unify it against the Roman government. His method was to offer his enemies friendship and alliance before maneuvering himself into position to bring them under his control (vv. 22–24). One of the kingdoms he tried to overtake was the Egyptian empire of the Ptolemies (vv. 25–27). During one of his invasions of Egypt (170), Antiochus was met outside Alexandria by a Roman commander named Popilius Laenas. Popilius informed Antiochus "that the Roman government ordered him to quit [his campaign against] Egypt immediately or face the consequences of war with Rome. Remembering what had happened to his father at the Battle of Magnesia and recalling also his years as a young hostage in Roman captivity, it did not take Antiochus very long to give way before this mandate."[7] However, this humiliation so angered Antiochus that he vented his rage on Jerusalem (v. 28) by storming the city and massacring 80,000 men, women, and

6. Whitcomb, *Daniel*, p. 150. More complete discussions of the conflicts between the Ptolemies and the Seleucids can be found in these sources: Archer, "Daniel," pp. 130–43; Pentecost, "Daniel," pp. 1368–70; John F. Walvoord, *Daniel: The Key to Prophetic Revelation* (Chicago: Moody Press, 1971), pp. 257–69.

7. Archer, "Daniel," p. 137.

children (2 Macc. 5:11–14). In 168, Antiochus returned to Jerusalem and desecrated the sanctuary by sacrificing swine on the altar and erecting a statue of the Olympian god Zeus (Dan. 11:31). This Syrian ruler also destroyed several scrolls of the Mosaic Law and forbade the practices of keeping the Sabbath, circumcising male children, and carrying out the official temple sacrifices decreed in the Law.[8] Those Jews who refused to submit to his orders were persecuted and martyred (vv. 32–33). However, after the Jewish Maccabaean family began to lead the revolt against Antiochus, the Seleucid forces eventually started to suffer some significant defeats, but not without the loss of many courageous Jews (vv. 34–35a). In 165, Judas Maccabaeus cleansed the Jerusalem temple and restored worship within its walls. But, as prophesied in the biblical text, the struggle against religious persecution did not end in the second century B.C.; it will continue until the " 'appointed time' " brings it to a close (v. 35b).

II. Some Significant Wars in the Future

Daniel 11:36–12:1 foretells some of what is to come under the Antichrist's reign during the Great Tribulation. Let's zero in on this section of Scripture.

A. The Antichrist's style. The Bible tells us that the Antichrist " 'will do as he pleases, and he will exalt and magnify himself above every god, and will speak monstrous things against the God of gods' " (11:36a). This satanically empowered ruler will be domineering and arrogant, and he will even set himself up as the Lord of lords and King of kings. In doing so, he will ignore his religious heritage and demand to be the sole object of people's worship (v. 37). The Antichrist will not desire female affection, and he "will lavish all his vast resources upon military fortifications and programs and will encourage cooperation by distributing positions of authority and valuable property to his followers"[9] (vv. 37a, 38–39).

B. The Antichrist's defeat. While the Antichrist is residing in Palestine, " 'the king of the South will collide with him, and the king of the North will storm against him with chariots, with horsemen, and with many ships; and he [i.e., the northern king] will enter countries, overflow them, and pass through' " (v. 40). The rulers in view here are the national leaders of an Egypt-based Arabian confederation and a political power far enough north of Palestine for its military to have to advance through other countries to get to Palestine. In our day, Russia fulfills the

---

8. See Archer, "Daniel," p. 139; Whitcomb, *Daniel*, p. 151; and Pentecost, "Daniel," p. 1370.

9. Whitcomb, *Daniel*, p. 155.

required criteria for the " 'king of the North.' " The text informs us that as the army of the North advances, it will defeat many countries and invade Palestine but fail to capture the Antichrist. It will also " 'gain control over the hidden treasures of gold and silver, and over all the precious things of Egypt,' " and continue its conquest into northeast Africa (vv. 41–43). While glorying in his victory, the ruler of the North will hear " 'rumors from the East and from the North' " (v. 44a), probably regarding a counterattack. In hopes of smashing the opposition, he will regroup his forces and launch out against his enemies " 'with great wrath' " (v. 44b). The text indicates that he will prepare for battle " 'between the seas [i.e., the Mediterranean Sea and the Dead Sea] and the beautiful Holy Mountain [i.e., Mount Moriah, where the temple will be]' " (v. 45a). No doubt, this last stand will be fought on the plain of Megiddo, or Jezreel, which is otherwise known as Armageddon (cf. Rev. 16:16). The Antichrist and his army, as well as the troops from the East (possibly China) and the West (the Roman confederacy and other Western nations), will assemble against the military of the North. Then the northern leader, his forces, and all the other armies present will be utterly crushed on this battlefield by Christ and the heavenly hosts (Dan. 11:45b–12:1; cf. Rev. 19:11–21). Indeed, the devastation will be so great that cities all over the world will be leveled, and entire geographic areas will be destroyed (Rev. 16:17–20). The only people on earth who will survive this expression of divine wrath will be those who become Christians during the Tribulation (Dan. 12:1).

III. Some Essential Applications for the Present

There will always be those who will doubt, even mock, the biblical teaching about the last days (2 Pet. 3:3–4). But, as the Apostle Peter says:

When they maintain this, it escapes their notice that by the word of God the heavens existed long ago and the earth was formed out of water and by water, through which the world at that time was destroyed, being flooded with water. But the present heavens and earth by His word are being reserved for fire, kept for the day of judgment and destruction of ungodly men. But do not let this one fact escape your notice, beloved, that with the Lord one day is as a thousand years, and a thousand years as one day. The Lord is not slow about His promise, as some count slowness, but is patient toward you, not wishing for any to perish but for all to come to repentance. But the day of the Lord will come like a thief, in which the heavens will pass away with a roar and the elements will be destroyed with intense heat and the earth and its works will be burned up. Since all these things are to be destroyed in this way, what sort of people ought you to be in holy conduct and godliness. (2 Pet. 3:5–11)

These sobering words suggest at least two applications we should make in our lives.

A. Realizing that the end is approaching, we should consistently strive to live godly lives.

B. Knowing that God's judgment is coming, we should diligently seek to spread the good news about Christ.

Living Insights

Study One ■■■■■■■■■■■■■■■■■■■■■■■■■■■■■■■■■■

Because the action is fast and furious in Daniel 11, it would be good for us to slow down and catch our breath.

● Take some time to *paraphrase* Daniel 11, just as you did in Daniel 2. As you read its forty-five verses, write them out in your own words. Some sections will be easier to paraphrase than others. The key is to discover and explore the feelings conveyed in these verses. If the entire chapter is too much to tackle all at once, seek a more attainable goal, such as the first twenty-eight verses.

Living Insights

Study Two ■■■■■■■■■■■■■■■■■■■■■■■■■■■■■■■■■■

Nuclear war—just the thought of it reduces everything to the basics. It raises issues of life and death ... the eternal and the temporal.

● Only two things on this earth will last forever: people and God's Word. What are you doing to invest your life in eternal values? Allow the questions below to prompt your thoughts toward personally applying the prophecy in Daniel 11.

—How am I investing my life in people?

—How can I be more effective in presenting Christ to others?

—How am I investing my life in the Word of God?

—How can I make the time I spend studying the Scriptures more valuable?

A Prophetic Quartet
Daniel 12:1–4

Over the centuries, God has revealed to mankind His pattern for the future. Sometimes He has unveiled large segments of this plan, whereas at other times He has provided only glimpses. Eventually, however, the Lord wrapped up His written revelation to man with the completion of the Apostle John's letter to the seven churches—namely, Revelation.[1] The twentieth chapter of this epistle contains some information that helps explain the events described in Daniel 12:1–4. Together, these passages clarify that there will be separate fates for believers and unbelievers once the Tribulation period comes to a close. Let's be attentive as we study the message of these passages, checking our hearts to be sure of our eternal destiny.

I. The Setting

We should recall that Daniel 12:1–4 falls on the heels of a prophecy concerning the seven-year Tribulation (Dan. 11:36–45). In fact, the first verse of chapter 12 states that during this time of divine judgment, the angel Michael will rise to defend and deliver the Jews—the people he has been assigned to protect. His ministry will come none too soon, since the Jews will be going through a terrible " 'time of distress' " (v. 1b). No period of persecution, suffering, or devastation has been or ever will be comparable to what will be unleashed during this time of hell on earth.

II. Four Groups of People and Their Destinies

Up to this point, the angel's message to Daniel has been a relatively bleak one. However, the prophecy given in the opening verses of chapter 12 predicts a time when God's people will be vindicated and His enemies judged. With regard to this truth, the angel revealed four groups of people.

A. " 'Everyone who is found written in the book.' " This phrase in Daniel 12:1b is clarified in Revelation 20:12. Here we learn that " 'the book' " is "the book of life"—a chronicle which lists the name of every human being who has ever trusted in Christ as Savior. The angel told Daniel that each Jew who places

---

1. Some excellent discussions on the development and compilation of the Bible can be found in these sources: R. Laird Harris, *Inspiration and Canonicity of the Bible* (Grand Rapids, Mich.: Zondervan Publishing House, 1969); Norman L. Geisler and William E. Nix, *From God to Us: How We Got Our Bible* (Chicago: Moody Press, 1974); Norman L. Geisler, "The Extent of the Old Testament Canon," in *Current Issues in Biblical and Patristic Interpretation,* edited by Gerald F. Hawthorne (Grand Rapids, Mich.: William B. Eerdmans Publishing Co., 1975), pp. 31–46.

his or her faith in Christ during the Tribulation will be preserved through that period and eventually delivered from it (Dan. 12:1b; cf. Rev. 7:2–8). These, and all other saints who survive the Tribulation, will be the ones who repopulate the earth during the Millennium.[2]

B. **" 'Those who sleep in the dust of the ground.' "** Daniel 12:2a discloses that all believers and unbelievers who have died will be bodily resurrected at the end of the Tribulation. Believers will be resurrected " 'to everlasting life' " with the Lord, while unbelievers will be raised from the grave " 'to disgrace and everlasting contempt' " apart from God (v. 2b). We know from the New Testament that the first group of believers to be resurrected will include only those who trusted in Christ during the Church Age (1 Thess. 4:14–17). This resurrection event will occur at the time of the Rapture. The second group of believers to be resurrected will be comprised of those saints who died prior to the Church Age and those who lost their lives during the Tribulation. They will be raised from their graves when Christ returns to earth to establish His Millennial Kingdom (Isa. 26:19–21; 1 Cor. 15:20–24, 51–57; Rev. 20:4–6). Following the thousand-year earthly reign of Christ, all deceased unbelievers will be resurrected and judged according to the deeds they performed while alive on earth (Rev. 20:5, 11–13). And since works cannot save anyone (cf. Rom. 3:21–30, Eph. 2:8–9), all unbelievers will be sentenced to everlasting punishment in hell (Matt. 25:41–46, 2 Thess. 1:6–9, Rev. 20:14–15). Concerning this awful separation from God, C. S. Lewis makes some insightful remarks:

> Though Our Lord often speaks of Hell as a sentence inflicted by a tribunal, He also says elsewhere that the judgement consists in the very fact that men prefer darkness to light, and that not He, but His "word," judges men. We are therefore at liberty— since the two conceptions, in the long run, mean the same thing—to think of this bad man's perdition not as a sentence imposed on him but as the mere fact of being what he is. The characteristic of lost souls is "their rejection of everything that is not simply themselves." Our imaginary egoist has tried to turn everything he meets into a province or appendage

2. Charles C. Ryrie develops this point and uses it to support a pretribulational view of the Rapture in his book titled *What You Should Know about the Rapture* (Chicago: Moody Press, 1981), chap. 9.

of the self. The taste for the *other*, that is, the very capacity for enjoying good, is quenched in him except in so far as his body still draws him into some rudimentary contact with an outer world. Death removes this last contact. He has his wish—to live wholly in the self and to make the best of what he finds there. And what he finds there is Hell.[3]

The chart at the end of this lesson illustrates the destinies of these four groups of people.

C. " 'Those who have insight.' " This phrase in Daniel 12:3a probably refers to those who will teach the Scriptures during the Tribulation (cf. 11:33, 35). It will take a great deal of courage and commitment to instruct people in God's Word while living under the rule of the Antichrist. Those who do " 'will shine brightly like the brightness of the expanse of heaven' " (12:3a). Because of their faithfulness in teaching the Bible during such an incredible time of persecution, these believers will be blessed in a special way, perhaps at the Second Advent of Christ.

D. " 'Those who lead the many to righteousness.' " In Daniel 12:3b, the people who fit this description are those who will evangelize the unsaved during the Tribulation. These individuals will spread the good news of salvation despite intense oppression and the threat of execution. As a result of their loyalty and bravery, they will be rewarded by God to the degree that they will shine " 'like the stars forever and ever' " (v. 3c). This too may occur at Christ's Second Coming.

III. A Command to Conceal

After describing these groups of people and their ultimate destinies, the angelic messenger directed Daniel to conceal the prophecy and seal up the Book of Daniel " 'until the end of time' " (v. 4a). The New Testament indicates that ever since the earthly ministry, death, and resurrection of Christ, we have been in the end times (Acts 2:15–17, Heb. 1:2, James 5:3, 1 Pet. 1:20). Therefore, it seems appropriate to understand the angel's command as being valid until the New Testament era. The words " 'many will go back and forth, and knowledge will increase' " (Dan. 12:4b) refer to the eager investigation and subsequent understanding of the prophecies revealed to Daniel. The angel was telling Daniel that, as time passed, serious students of his book would gain a clearer picture of what it teaches and how and when its prophecies would be fulfilled. This, of course, was made possible when the Lord finished revealing His written

---

3. C. S. Lewis, *The Problem of Pain* (New York: Macmillan Publishing Co., 1962), pp. 122–23.

Word to man in the first century B.C.[4] And among the books He inspired, Revelation is the best commentary on the end-time prophecies given in the Book of Daniel. Now we have what we need to gain a more knowledgeable comprehension of that which Daniel longed to grasp (cf. Dan. 12:8–9).

IV. Some Truths to Live By

Many comforting predictions for both Jewish and Gentile Christians are compressed into Daniel 12:1–4. Interwoven through these prophecies of the future are three principles that can encourage us in the present.

A. Man honors the famous and soon forgets them, but God honors the unknown and never forgets them. Hebrews 6:10 states, "God is not unjust so as to forget your work and the love which you have shown toward His name, in having ministered and in still ministering to the saints." Here on earth, we may never get to stand under the spotlight and receive the applause of man. Even if such an opportunity were to come, we would not be remembered by many for very long. God, on the other hand, sees everything we do, and He will one day abundantly reward us for our faithfulness to Him.

B. Man gives his rewards now, but God saves His until later. How much better it is to receive an imperishable reward from the Lord when we are in heaven with Him instead of a corruptible one from man while we are still strangers on earth (cf. Matt. 6:19–21, Heb. 11:13–16).

C. Man's methods are connected with time, but God's are connected with eternity. The perspectives of man are generally short-sighted and his ways usually self-centered. The Lord, however, sees every detail of the past, present, and future, and He is carefully fulfilling His plan according to His all-good will.

---

4. Most contemporary Bible scholars believe that the books of the New Testament were written before A.D. 100. In recent years, John A. T. Robinson, a Bible critic who once claimed post-first-century dates for some New Testament books, now convincingly argues that the New Testament was completed by A.D. 70. The evidence supporting his revised stance is provided in his book titled *Redating the New Testament* (Philadelphia: The Westminster Press, 1976).

A Survey of the Resurrections

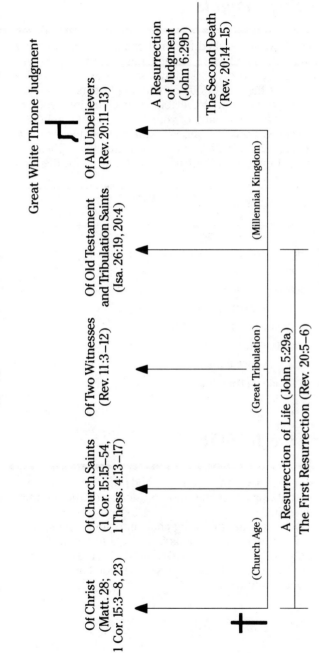

Of Christ
(Matt. 28;
1 Cor. 15:3–8, 23)

Of Church Saints
(1 Cor. 15:15–54,
1 Thess. 4:13–17)

Of Two Witnesses
(Rev. 11:3–12)

Of Old Testament
and Tribulation Saints
(Isa. 26:19, 20:4)

Great White Throne Judgment

Of All Unbelievers
(Rev. 20:11–13)

A Resurrection
of Judgment
(John 6:29b)

The Second Death
(Rev. 20:14–15)

(Church Age)

(Great Tribulation)

(Millennial Kingdom)

A Resurrection of Life (John 5:29a)

The First Resurrection (Rev. 20:5–6)

115

Living Insights

Study One ▬▬▬▬▬▬▬▬▬▬▬▬▬▬▬▬▬▬▬▬▬▬▬▬▬▬▬▬

Now that we've reached the final chapter of Daniel, we would be wise to look back on all we've studied. Let's reexamine the first six chapters of Daniel in these two Living Insights, and then review the last six chapters at the end of our concluding lesson.

- Once you've copied the following chart into your notebook, turn back to the beginning of your study guide, notebook, and the Book of Daniel. Look for one key spiritual or doctrinal truth in each of the first nine lessons. Since we'll search for applications later, center your attention on the truths you found to be the most meaningful.

Daniel 1–6	
Lesson Titles	Meaningful Truths
Prophecy in Panorama	
How to Pass a Test without Cheating	
A King on a Couch	
A Blueprint of Tomorrow	
A Ragtime Band and a Fiery Furnace	
Insomnia, Insanity, and Insight	
The Handwriting on the Wall	
The Marks of Integrity	
The Lions in Daniel's Den	

 Living Insights

Study Two ▬▬▬▬▬▬▬▬▬▬▬▬▬▬▬▬▬▬▬▬▬▬▬▬▬▬

One of the most important methods of learning is review. Educators agree that it is a valuable tool for increasing the retention of what you have learned.

- As you copy the following chart into your notebook, you will notice we've redirected our focus from facts to applications. What did you apply to your life from Daniel 1–6? Single out one principle or activity from each lesson listed that you have sought to make a part of your walk with God.

Daniel 1–6	
Lesson Titles	Significant Applications
Prophecy in Panorama	
How to Pass a Test without Cheating	
A King on a Couch	
A Blueprint of Tomorrow	
A Ragtime Band and a Fiery Furnace	
Insomnia, Insanity, and Insight	
The Handwriting on the Wall	
The Marks of Integrity	
The Lions in Daniel's Den	

The End of the Age

Daniel 12:5–13

The Book of Daniel begins with the siege of Jerusalem and the capture and exile of many Jews to Babylon. As the book comes to a close, it reveals a future period in which the Jews will be persecuted by the Antichrist and purged by God. Although this ancient account also foretells a time at which Jewish believers will be vindicated and rewarded, its description of the awful torment they will experience prompted Daniel to inquire further about the end of the age. What he was told provides not only a fitting conclusion to the book but also some practical counsel to apply.

I. Introductory Comments

The final nine verses of the Book of Daniel are part of the theological and prophetic section of the book—chapters 7 through 12. The first six chapters also contain these characteristics, but their focus is largely biographical and historical. Daniel 12:5–13, moreover, is part of a lengthy vision that the prophet Daniel sees while standing on the bank of the Tigris River (10:1, 4). He received this vision from God as an answer to his fervent prayers concerning the future of the Jews (vv. 2–3, 12; 11:16, 28–12:3).

II. Expository Remarks

As we look over Daniel 12:5–13, we can see that it contains four major elements. Let's examine each one as we seek to understand these closing verses.

A. The individuals involved. Besides Daniel, there are two unidentified figures that speak in this text. Each of them is said to be standing on opposite banks of the Tigris River (v. 5). Since Daniel has been dialoguing with angels throughout this vision, we can safely assume that these two new characters were angels as well. However, one of them may not have been an ordinary angel. For the text states that one of these beings "was above the waters of the river" (v. 7a)—an indication that this angel possessed great power and authority over nature. We know that the Lord frequently gives angels the authority to exercise their suprahuman power in order to carry out certain aspects of His plan (cf. Ps. 103:20–21, Heb. 1:14). But He seldom grants them permission to control the elements of nature; when He does, it is usually in relationship to meting out judgment (cf. Rev. 7:1, 16:1–12).[1] Therefore, if the being above the water in Daniel 12:7

---

1. For a thorough biblical treatment of angels, see C. Fred Dickason's book *Angels, Elect and Evil* (Chicago: Moody Press, 1975).

was not an ordinary angel, it may have been an angelic manifestation of the Son of God. There is an angel called "the angel of the Lord" who appears a number of times in the Old Testament. He is referred to and worshiped as deity (cf. Gen. 16:7–13, Judg. 13:15–23). During His earthly ministry, Jesus Christ called Himself the same name that this angel had claimed—namely, "I Am," the proper name of God (cf. John 8:58 with Exod. 3:2–6, 13–15).[2] If one of the angels with Daniel was the angel of the Lord, then Daniel was conversing directly with the preincarnate Christ.

B. **The questions asked.** Two questions are posed in Daniel 12:5–13. The first one was spoken by the lesser angel to the superior one (v. 6a). He asked, " 'How long will it be until the end of these wonders?' " (v. 6b). This angel wanted to know the length of the disciplinary period Israel would experience during the Great Tribulation. The second question was also posed to the superior angel, but this time by Daniel (v. 8a). His query was, " 'What will be the outcome of these events?' " (v. 8b). Daniel longed to know what would finally happen to his people after they had been delivered from the Tribulation.

C. **The answers given.** The superior angel responded to both questions in the order they were given. Let's look at each answer.

    1. **The length of time.** The angel said that Israel's period of chastisement would last " 'for a time, times, and a half a time' " (v. 7b). This is a reference to the same 3½-year period that was earlier revealed to Daniel concerning the Antichrist's persecution of believers during the Tribulation (7:25). This outbreak of violent hatred toward God's people will begin when the Antichrist breaks his covenant with the Jewish people in the middle of the seven-year Tribulation (9:27a). It will come to an end " 'as soon as they finish shattering the power of the holy people' " (12:7c; cf. v. 10). As John C. Whitcomb explains:

> The Beast and the False Prophet will be God's visible agents (through Satan) to accomplish this "strange work" of crushing the pride and self-sufficiency of Israel, so that she, as a last resort, will cry out, "Blessed is He who comes in the name of the Lord" (Matt. 23:39), and will enter

---

2. See Dickason, *Angels,* chap. 6, for a helpful discussion on the identity of the angel of the Lord as the preincarnate Son of God.

into her millennial rest, having "received of the Lord's hand double for all her sins" (Isa. 40:2).[3]

In Daniel 12:11–12, we find more specifics concerning this time of divine discipline on Israel. The superior angel predicted that " 'from the time that the regular sacrifice is abolished, and the abomination of desolation is set up, there will be 1,290 days' " (v. 11). If a Jewish calendar year was 360 days, this period comes out to be 3½ years, plus thirty days. The angel never gave the reason for the extra thirty days, and Bible commentators vary greatly in their explanations of this addition. Perhaps the added days will be needed for the clean-up operations that will take place after the Battle of Armageddon (cf. Ezek. 39:11–16; Rev. 14:19–20, 19:17–21). Another possibility is that the thirty days will be a period in which the Jerusalem temple will be thoroughly cleansed of the abominations committed in it by the Antichrist.[4] To the thirty extra days, the angel added forty-five more (Dan. 12:12). The speculation among Bible scholars regarding these additional days is also quite varied. It is possible, however, that these days will be necessary to prepare for the initiation of Christ's millennial reign on earth.

2. **The final outcome.** In response to Daniel's question concerning the Jews' future after the Tribulation, the superior angel said, " 'Go your way, Daniel, for these words are concealed and sealed up until the end time' " (v. 9). To this the angel added, " 'But as for you, go your way to the end [of your life]; then you will enter into rest and rise again for your allotted portion at the end of the age' " (v. 13). Commenting on this verse, John Whitcomb writes:

> After the "rest" of an intermediate state (between death and resurrection; see 1 Sam. 28:15), which will continue for righteous Jews until "the end of the age" (i.e., the end of the Great Tribulation), Daniel will "rise again" and will enjoy his "lot" (i.e., inheritance; cf. Col. 1:12) during the Kingdom age. He will share this infinite privilege with all "first resurrection" people who "will be priests of God and of Christ and will reign with Him for a thousand years" (Rev. 20:6) over the present earth and then

3. John C. Whitcomb, *Daniel*, Everyman's Bible Commentary (Chicago: Moody Press, 1985), p. 166.

4. See Whitcomb, *Daniel*, p. 168.

forever in the new heavens and the new earth
that God will create for His people (Rev. 21–22).[5]
In the meantime, however, the angel's counsel to Daniel
was: "Carry on. Be about your business. Don't be so
concerned about the future that you neglect your present
responsibilities." Throughout the history of the Church,
there have been many Christians who have failed to accept this advice. One such group of believers lived in
Thessalonica during the first century A.D. They had heard
that Christ had already come and established His Kingdom
on earth (1 Thess. 2:2). Apparently, some of them used this
news to excuse themselves from work and to engage in
gossip (3:11–12). The Apostle Paul strongly rebuked their
response to this unfounded message (vv. 14–15) and
corrected their theology, reminding them of what he had
taught them about the last days (2:3–12). We would be wise
to heed the counsel that the angel gave to Daniel: *Seek to
maintain a biblical balance between looking forward to the
future and living in the present.*

III. Applicatory Principles

From our study in the Book of Daniel, we can see at least three
truths of timeless relevance that emerge from their historical and
predictive details.

**A. The more time we spend with God, the more teach-
able we become concerning Him.**

**B. The more questions we ask God, the more dependent
we become on Him.**

**C. The more truth we discover about God, the more
profound He becomes to us.**

 Living Insights

Study One ▬▬▬▬▬▬▬▬▬▬▬▬▬▬▬▬▬▬▬▬▬▬▬▬▬▬▬▬▬▬▬

We began the process of review in our last lesson. Let's continue to
refresh our memories as we reflect on the last half of Daniel's great
book. What did God teach you through our study of Daniel 7–12?

- The following chart, like the one in the previous lesson, can be
  copied into your notebook. By reviewing your study guide, notebook,
  and Bible, recall at least one significant truth from each lesson.

Continued on next page

---

5. Whitcomb, *Daniel*, p. 168.

Daniel 7–12	
Lesson Titles	Meaningful Truths
A Prophetic Collage	
The Final World Dictator	
The Living End	
True Confessions	
The Backbone of Biblical Prophecy	
Demons between Heaven and Earth	
Wars and Rumors of War	
A Prophetic Quartet	
The End of the Age	

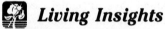

Living Insights

Study Two

It's helpful to reflect on the doctrinal truths we have studied, but we also want to pay attention to their application in our lives. So let's review the things God has been teaching us.

- Look over the last nine lessons and answer the following question: What one application did I make from this lesson that truly affected my life?

Daniel 7–12	
Lesson Titles	Significant Applications
A Prophetic Collage	
The Final World Dictator	
The Living End	
True Confessions	
The Backbone of Biblical Prophecy	
Demons between Heaven and Earth	
Wars and Rumors of War	
A Prophetic Quartet	
The End of the Age	

Acknowledgments

Insight for Living is grateful for permission to quote from the following sources:

Archer, Gleason L., Jr. "Daniel." In *The Expositor's Bible Commentary.* 12 vols. Edited by Frank E. Gaebelein. Grand Rapids, Mich.: Regency Reference Library, Zondervan Publishing House, 1976– . Vol. 7.

Baldwin, Joyce G. *Daniel: An Introduction and Commentary.* Tyndale OT Commentaries. Downers Grove, Ill.: InterVarsity Press, 1978.

Hoekema, Anthony A. "Amillennialism." In *The Meaning of the Millennium: Four Views.* Edited by Robert G. Clouse. Downers Grove, Ill.: InterVarsity Press, 1977.

Keil, C. F. *Biblical Commentary on the Book of Daniel.* Translated by M. G. Easton. Grand Rapids, Mich.: William B. Eerdmans Publishing Co., n.d.

Lewis, C. S. *The Problem of Pain.* New York: Macmillan Publishing Co., 1962.

Pentecost, J. Dwight. "Daniel." In *The Bible Knowledge Commentary: Old Testament Edition.* Edited by John F. Walvoord and Roy B. Zuck. Wheaton, Ill.: Victor Books, 1985.

Unger, Merrill F. "Vision." In *Unger's Bible Dictionary.* 3d ed., rev. Chicago: Moody Press, 1966.

Vos, Howard F. *Archaeology in Bible Lands.* Chicago: Moody Press, 1977.

Walvoord, John F. *Daniel: The Key to Prophetic Revelation.* Chicago: Moody Press, 1971.

White, William, Jr. "Babylon, City of." In *The New International Dictionary of Biblical Archaeology.* Grand Rapids, Mich.: Regency Reference Library, Zondervan Publishing House, 1983.

Whitcomb, John C. *Daniel.* Everyman's Bible Commentary. Chicago: Moody Press, 1985.

Wood, Leon. *A Survey of Israel's History.* Grand Rapids, Mich.: Zondervan Publishing House, 1970.

Insight for Living
Cassette Tapes
DANIEL
GOD'S PATTERN FOR THE FUTURE

Interesting, intriguing, inviting . . . these words describe the appeal of this twelve-chapter book of prophecy. The man and his message stand out as significant statements, offering hope for today and insight into the future. A *must* for those who wish to understand God's prophetic plan for the world.

			U.S.	Canadian
DAN	CS	Cassette series—includes album cover	$50.25	$63.75
		Individual cassettes—include messages		
		A and B	5.00	6.35

These prices are effective as of May 1986 and are subject to change.

DAN 1-A: *Prophecy in Panorama*—Selected Scripture
   B: *How to Pass a Test without Cheating*—Daniel 1

DAN 2-A: *A King on the Couch*—Daniel 2:1–30
   B: *A Blueprint of Tomorrow*—Daniel 2:31–49

DAN 3-A: *A Ragtime Band and a Fiery Furnace*—Daniel 3, 1 Peter 2:18–20
   B: *Insomnia, Insanity, and Insight*—Daniel 4

DAN 4-A: *The Handwriting on the Wall*—Daniel 5
   B: *The Marks of Integrity*—Daniel 6:1–16a

DAN 5-A: *The Lions in Daniel's Den*—Daniel 6:16b–28
   B: *A Prophetic Collage*—Daniel 7

DAN 6-A: *The Final World Dictator*—Selected Scripture
   B: *The Living End*—Daniel 8

DAN 7-A: *True Confessions*—Daniel 9:1–19
   B: *The Backbone of Biblical Prophecy*—Daniel 9:24–27

DAN 8-A: *Demons between Heaven and Earth*—Daniel 10
   B: *Wars and Rumors of War*—Daniel 11:1–12:1

DAN 9-A: *A Prophetic Quartet*—Daniel 12:1–4
   B: *The End of the Age*—Daniel 12:5–13

Ordering Information

U.S. ordering information: You are welcome to use our toll-free number (for Visa and MasterCard orders only) between the hours of 8:30 A.M. and 4:00 P.M., Pacific Time, Monday through Friday. The number is **(800) 772-8888.** This number may be used anywhere in the continental United States excluding California, Hawaii, and Alaska. Orders from those areas are handled through our Sales Department at **(714) 870-9161.** We are unable to accept collect calls.

Your order will be processed promptly. We ask that you allow four to six weeks for delivery by fourth-class mail. If you wish your order to be shipped first-class, please add 10 percent of the total order (not including California sales tax) for shipping and handling.

Canadian ordering information: Your order will be processed promptly. We ask that you allow approximately four weeks for delivery by first-class mail to the U.S./Canadian border. All orders will be shipped from our office in Fullerton, California. For our listeners in British Columbia, a 7 percent sales tax must be added to the total of all tape orders (not including first-class postage). For further information, please contact our office at **(604) 272-5811.**

Payment options: We accept personal checks, money orders, Visa, and MasterCard in payment for materials ordered. Unfortunately, we are unable to offer invoicing or COD orders. If the amount of your check or money order is less than the amount of your purchase, your check will be returned so that you may place your order again with the correct amount. All orders must be paid in full before shipment can be made.

Returned checks: There is a $10 charge for any returned check (regardless of the amount of your order) to cover processing and invoicing.

Guarantee: Our tapes are guaranteed for ninety days against faulty performance or breakage due to a defect in the tape. For best results, please be sure your tape recorder is in good operating condition and is cleaned regularly.

Mail your order to one of the following addresses:

Insight for Living	Insight for Living Ministries
Sales Department	Post Office Box 2510
Post Office Box 4444	Vancouver, BC
Fullerton, CA 92634	Canada V6B 3W7

Quantity discounts and gift certificates are available upon request.

Overseas ordering information is provided on the reverse side of the order form.

Order Form

Please send me the following cassette tapes:

The current series: ☐ DAN CS Daniel: God's Pattern for the Future
Individual cassettes: ☐ DAN 1 ☐ DAN 2 ☐ DAN 3
☐ DAN 4 ☐ DAN 5 ☐ DAN 6
☐ DAN 7 ☐ DAN 8 ☐ DAN 9

I am enclosing:

$ _____ To purchase the cassette series for $50.25 (in Canada $63.75*) which includes the album cover

$ _____ To purchase individual tapes at $5.00 each (in Canada $6.35*)

$ _____ Total of purchases

$ _____ California residents please add 6 percent sales tax

$ _____ U.S. residents please add 10 percent for first-class shipping and handling if desired

$ _____ *British Columbia residents please add 7 percent sales tax

$ _____ Canadian residents please add 6 percent for postage

$ _____ **Overseas residents please add appropriate postage** (See postage chart under "Overseas Ordering Information.")

$ _____ As a gift to the Insight for Living radio ministry for which a tax-deductible receipt will be issued

$ _____ **Total amount due (Please do not send cash.)**

Form of payment:

☐ Check or money order made payable to Insight for Living
☐ Credit card (Visa or MasterCard only)
If there is a balance: ☐ apply it as a donation   ☐ please refund

---

Credit card purchases:

☐ Visa   ☐ MasterCard number _____
Expiration date _____
Signature _____

We cannot process your credit card purchase without your signature.

Name _____

Address _____

_____

City _____

State/Province _____ Zip/Postal code _____

Country _____

Telephone (_____) _____ Radio station __ __ __ __

Should questions arise concerning your order, we may need to contact you.

Overseas Ordering Information

If you do not live in the United States or Canada, please note the following information. This will ensure efficient processing of your request.

Estimated time of delivery: We ask that you allow approximately twelve to sixteen weeks for delivery by surface mail. If you would like your order sent airmail, the length of delivery may be reduced. All orders will be shipped from our office in Fullerton, California.

Payment options: Due to fluctuating currency rates, we can accept only personal checks made payable in U.S. funds, international money orders, Visa, and MasterCard in payment for materials ordered. If the amount of your check or money order is less than the amount of your purchase, your check will be returned so that you may place your order again with the correct amount. All orders must be paid in full before shipment can be made.

Returned checks: There is a $10 charge for any returned check (regardless of the amount of your order) to cover processing and invoicing.

Postage and handling: Please add to the amount purchased the basic postage cost for the service you desire. All orders must include postage based on the chart below.

Purchase Amount		Surface Postage	Airmail Postage
From	To	Percentage of Order	Percentage of Order
$ .01	$15.00	40%	75%
15.01	75.00	25%	45%
75.01	or more	15%	40%

Guarantee: Our tapes are guaranteed for ninety days against faulty performance or breakage due to a defect in the tape. For best results, please be sure your tape recorder is in good operating condition and is cleaned regularly.

Mail your order or inquiry to the following address:

Insight for Living
Sales Department
Post Office Box 4444
Fullerton, CA 92634

Quantity discounts and gift certificates are available upon request.